I0772505

Your Boyfriend's Hooker

Stories of Men with Sex Workers

Lauren Brim, Ph.D.

All of the names have been changed to protect the identities of the
men who shared their stories.

Table of Contents

Introduction

This all began several years ago in the Malibu home of my then-boyfriend when I learned that he had received a hand job from a sex worker in Germany a year following his divorce. *You did what?* I thought. A barrage of questions followed. I was truly and deeply shocked. But why was I so shocked? I realized then that I had this idea that no one *I dated* would ever see a sex worker. That was something only those 'bad men' did. Was I alone in this assumption? Or was my then-boyfriend just an anomaly and my view about men could remain the same?

I set out contacting all of my ex-boyfriends to ask them to tell me about their experiences with sex workers. Instead of asking, "Have you ever been with a sex worker?" I said, "Tell me about your experiences with sex workers." Some hesitated, but most did not, and almost every single one of them had a story. And the stories were not what I would have thought. Some of them didn't like it and never did it again, and others enjoyed it. But were all women in denial like myself that men were paying for sex? And why was paying for sex considered such a bad thing? The idea never left me, and I continued to ask men I would meet in bars or at parties about their experiences with sex workers.

At long last I was in graduate school and completing a Doctorate in Human Sexuality, a subject that never ceased to fascinate and delight me, and I had the choice between conducting research into the impact of sexual education on female sexual response, or a qualitative assessment of the experiences of men with female sex workers. Guess which one I chose? You guessed it- men with sex workers! I completed my dissertation and it changed my life. After hours and hours of listening to these men tell me, not only about their stories with sex workers, but their desires, insecurities, fears, longings, and deepest conflicts, I promised them that I would take their stories out to the public where they could be seen, heard, and hopefully understood.

So here I present you with thirteen stories of men with sex workers. May they enlighten, touch, amuse, frighten, arouse, and even open your heart. And perhaps you will see what I saw, and realize that men are far different than we've been brought up to believe. The stereotype of the sex-hungry, emotionally vacant, always erect, violent man preying on hookers is so far from the truth it will shock and confuse you. If men aren't like that, then who are they? What do they want from women and from sex? And what about your boyfriend's hooker? Let's discover who she is together in these pages. It's time that male sexuality be seen and embraced for what it truly is, and human sexuality be taken out of the shadows of shame and secrecy, and into the light of conscious, curious, and unbiased investigation. It is only then that we will all have the freedom to be who we are, and conduct ourselves in the world with authenticity, integrity and love.

Agustín

Argentina, 1987

Well what I did is something really typical in my country. Actually my two brothers started like that, and most of the guys I know. It's a way in which many boys become men. I think it's different from a guy that goes to a prostitute today. I have some friends who still go to prostitutes and they have different reasons for it than I had. In my case, I was 14 years old when I had my first failed attempt with a prostitute. My friends told me that Santi, a mutual friend had already had sex and he was our age.

"So Santi is going to take us tomorrow night to a whore house," they told me. At that time it was usually your older brother or your dad who would take you to become a man. I was really, really happy to go, of course. I was 14 years old and my dick was up to my chin all the time and I wanted to know about it. So I was at home having lunch that day with my parents and my two younger brothers, singing, "Today I'm going to fu-ck. Today I'm going to fu-ck," and I see my mom and dad are trying to keep themselves from laughing. I never had any problems talking about those things with my parents. Years later I would tell my mom,

"Mom, I'm leaving for a couple of days, so tell Dad I took his condoms." I thought, I think it's appropriate to tell him and not have my dad open the drawer and say, "Oh, those fucking kids."

So my dad, before I go, takes me aside and says, "Agustín, you know that my first time was with a prostitute as well, so I can tell you my experience. If you want the money, I give you the money to go, no problem, but my experience is that it is better if you wait and you meet a girl, and you like her and she likes you. If you like each other it's going to be much, much nicer than with this woman whose only interest is in your money and she doesn't care about you."

"Okay, okay, I hear you, but give me the money," I replied. So he gave me the money and that night we were looking for the place and the guy leading the six or seven of us couldn't find it. So we approached another guy who was walking down the street and ask, "I'm sorry sir, but do you know where such-and-such a street is?"

"What are you looking for?" he asks.

"Oh, we have to go to meet a friend." So he tells us where to go and we follow the directions and get lost again and run into the same guy, and this time my friend says, "I'm sorry sir, we can't find the street. Where is the whore house?"

"I thought you were looking for that," he laughs. You go to the corner and it's on the left.

So we go to the corner and to the left and as we're about to go in, one of the guys walking out of the place yells to us,

"Keep walking, keep walking, keep walking. Don't go in!"

"What happened?" we say to him.

"Keep going!" he shouts back. And when we get to the corner and he says, "There is a truck from the government over there, and that car is flashing lights. I think they are cops."

"Oh, come on, you're paranoid," we tell him.

"No, no, I think they are cops, and you know, we shouldn't be there if they're going to raid the place."

"Dude, you're paranoid."

"No," he insists. So we go to eat a pizza across the street. We eat and have fun for an hour and a half and then we say, "Okay, let's go to have sex." So we go there, and the place is closed by the police. So it was a raid, and if we had gone there our parents would have gotten a call in the middle of the night saying, "You need to come to the police station to pick up your kid." So that didn't work out. My friends ended up going some time after that, but I didn't go with them. For some reason, after a little while, the words of my dad stayed in my head.

Two years later, it was spring of '87, and there's a free day from school and it's called Lover's Day or Student Day and everyone goes to picnic in the parks. The day before there was a 24 hour disco and I got some free entrance passes and went with some friends. We were waiting in line for three or four hours to get in, and we finally say, "Okay, we can't take it anymore, let's get the fuck out of here. Fuck this place." We were living 20 kilometers from the center, so we got on a bus. These friends of mine had been having parties on the weekends and calling prostitutes and all of that, and wanted to go to one that night, but I said, "No, I'm going to wait until I meet a girl," because the words my Dad said had stayed in my head.

"Okay, Agustín," they said, "but we're horny, and at the next stop there is a brothel and we're going to go. Are you going to keep traveling alone, or are you going to come with us?"

"Ah, shit. Okay, I'm coming with you."

So I go with them and we arrive at this shitty, shitty place, and my friend tells me "Okay, so basically, you see the girls and you go choose one and say to her, "Okay, let's go," and tell her it's your first time, because some girls, they treat you special when it's your first time, and you go upstairs and you do it." But I looked around and I didn't like any of the girls. There was one who was just okay, and my friend took her. So he goes up and I say to myself, *No, fuck it, I'm going to wait until he comes back,* because I don't like any of the other girls. So I wait and my friend comes back and says,

"So did you do it?"

"No, I was waiting for the girl that you took." So I go to her and say, "Let's go," and we go to the room upstairs and I tell her it's my first time.

"Okay," she says. She didn't give a shit. And then she says to me, "You want normal, común, or special?" and she gives me the price and I'm thinking, *Give me diesel,* but I ask her,

"What's the special?"

"I give you a blow job," she says.

"Well, it's my first time, so let's do it with all of the things." So I go to the bed and she starts giving me a blow job and at a certain point she just stops and she's going to sit on top of me and I say, "Wait, wait, I'm going to put on a condom," but she was ready to go on top of me with no condom. I guess she knew it was my first time so other than callouses she wouldn't get anything. So I put the condom on and she lays down on her back and I start going and at a certain moment I come, but I keep moving and it was my first time so I don't say anything. I'm not even changing the speed, and I think, *I could go for a second one. Two for the price of one.* So I keep going and going, but then at a certain point I think, *Maybe I am taking too long.* I don't know what is a normal length of time for this. And if she actually wants to check now and asks me to come out, she will see that I have come because its on the condom. But I keep going and I'm thinking, *Fuck,* and now I cannot come again because I'm thinking this. *Fuck, what do I do?* I cannot just stop. If she sees that I already came she's going to call the guys outside and I'm going to have the shit beat out of me because I don't have money for two, so I have to do something and I think, *Fuck, I cannot just stop.* So it's my first time having sex, and I decide to fake my orgasm. Yes, I faked an orgasm my first time, with a prostitute, who couldn't care less.

A year later we went, a group of friends, to another brothel. That was my second time with a prostitute and only my second time having sex. I was 17, and this time I chose a girl that I liked and it was much nicer. She said to me,
"Oh, your eyes are so beautiful," and she looked so happy, so I thought, *Maybe I can get something extra.* So after we finished the first round, she turned her body away from me and said, "Okay, a freebie," because she liked me. We did it doggie style. I wanted to put it in her ass, but she didn't want it in there. "No, no, no," she said, "not in the ass."

One year later, I had my first experience with a normal girl, and it was so much more fun. I could do so many things because I wasn't thinking, *Oh, I don't want to put my mouth there.* After that I realized I could get girls if I wanted to and it wasn't so difficult. When I was little, I was really shy, so it took me some time to become confident. And with time I got better and better at sex. Eventually I even got recommendations. "So-and-so told me I have to try you," the girls would say. I guess I was doing something right.

I have a friend who is married and I ask him,

"So how is it being married for so many years? Is it okay? Can you be faithful?" and he said,

"Look, every now and then it's good to have something on the side, but you have to pay. Because when you pay, it's a commercial transaction, so there are no feelings involved." So basically he told me he would go to prostitutes every now and then because he needs some refreshment – he needs something different. And when he comes back home he feels even closer and has more desire for his wife, like he appreciates it more. That's his view. Another friend of mine, I met him for a coffee in December and he said, "I was just with a whore." And he told me he goes over there because his wife was very jealous all the time for no reason and finally he said to himself, "Okay, you want to be jealous, I'm going to give you a reason to be jealous." So every now and then he goes with a younger girl that he likes and is more beautiful and now when she complains at least he know she has something to complain about. She doesn't know, of course, but he's not suffering inside saying, "Fuck, I didn't do anything and now she's breaking my balls. At least now she has a reason."

Us guys, we have a lot of pressure to know about sex. The women say, "It's okay, I'll teach you," but it's shameful that we don't know. A man should know. And the other factor is our hormones at that age. We have our cock up to our chin. I remember we were talking, a group of teenage guys, about how many times a day we would jerk off, and one guy said there was a day he did it 16 times. It's an age where it's like that. So the need of being a man and growing and experiencing things that adults experience, and the need of saying, "I did it. I'm not a virgin anymore," is so strong. You know that if you face a girl you at least have some experience and you know where everything goes. So boys feel pressure and they feel like they have to do it. I don't know if the boys do it today because the girls are fast now. The girls at my time, ages 14 or 16, they did nothing sexually! So many boys these days are with girls and starting in a much nicer way, because it is nicer when you do it with someone you care about, or at least someone who, if you're horny, is horny with you. Because boys at that age would even do it with a girl they don't like. It's just about having sex.

We have sayings about that, like, "If she's not beautiful, just put a flag around her face and you do it for the country," or "Even a hole in the wall is doable." But there's a point at which that ends. I remember when I was 26 years old and I felt something I never wanted to feel ever again, which was just after sex, I wanted the woman to go away. I said to myself, *I never want to feel that again.* And since then, whenever I felt that I wouldn't want to spend the night with the girl that I was with, I wouldn't have sex with her. Just doing it for the sake of doing it – no thank you. I enjoy the connection. It's not the moment you put it in and you come. It's the whole thing, from the first kiss to waking up and having breakfast, or not, but it's a whole thing that you share, in which a part of that, or several parts of that, are sex. I enjoy the talking in bed a lot. It's when you get to know the other person because you're naked literally and figuratively and you open more to the person in those moments. To me, that's really, really nice. What would I tell my son if I had one? I would say to him the same thing my dad said to me. "Maybe I would add, at least if you don't love her and she doesn't love you, then both of you should want to do it. Because you want to enjoy it. But yeah, wait and do it with someone you like." That's what I would tell him.

Phil

San Francisco, 1984

So I'm drinking heavily and I'm really excited to be in my favorite city of San Francisco. My brother lived in the Tenderloin, and I'm 18 or 19 living it up in this particular bar I went to. Maybe I'm underage, I don't know. So I'm drinking there and I walk down to the corner and there's prostitutes there, because, you know, it's the Tenderloin. Usually I'd see them and they didn't do much for me. Generally prostitutes are not runway models, at least the ones on the street aren't. So I don't know if I had a lot of drinks or not, but there I am on the corner and I see one on a mountain bike. She's blond and she doesn't look awful, and what really intrigued me was a sex worker on a mountain bike. So I can't remember how the conversation went with her but she knew pretty well what to do. So she tells me that we'll go down a little ways, and there's this private bookstore and we can go in this little room. "I know the guy," she tells me.

So if you've never been to these adult book stores, there's usually a little booth and before internet, you'd put coins in to watch the TV in there, and there's a curtain you can pull closed, and it's not bigger than a telephone booth. There's a bench and there's a TV across from the bench, and you can figure out what goes on from there. Typically, one of the things it's used most for is for men to connect and have oral sex. So men who haven't had encounters much, it's probably been in an adult bookstore. So it's San Francisco, there's a plethora of these, so we go to one just down the street, walk through the door, and she waves at the guy behind the counter and takes me in one of these booths. And it's like, she's busy. She's on the clock. And I'm nervous, like school boy giddy, and I don't do this often, but I could relate to people who get scared and start laughing. I remember white water rafting and this girl was just terrified and I asked her, "Why were you laughing when we were falling into the river?" and she said, "I was just scared." So it was kind of like that, I was giggling and laughing like, this is surreal, I can't believe this is happening. What the hell am I going to do?

I think she said it was 40 dollars. "Twenty for head and forty for the whole deal." So she's going right to business. It's like a production for her and for me I'm just like, I can't believe this is happening. So she starts pulling my pants down and I'm sitting on this bench, and she puts a condom on me and she starts doing oral sex. I remember the room was orange or red and there were probably a rack of greeting cards like six feet away. And I'm laughing so I can't get much of an erection, cause you know, it's so surreal. So she's kind of working it, doing her thing, and now I'm more embarrassed and laughing because I don't have an erection. I don't even know how she managed to put a condom on, but she's doing that.

And so while she's doing this, she keeps telling me the floor is messy and she doesn't want my pants to get in it. So she keeps telling me she's holding my pants up off the floor, cause they're at my knees or something. And I have no idea what's going on, just, "Okay, this is what we do." And I could understand the floor being gooey and messy. Later on I figure out what this was about. So the she stands up and kind of bends over a little bit and grabs the wall and I stand up and she puts me inside her. And I'm still in this surreal thing, I don't have an erection, I'm not just going at it, like, oh, this is great, I've got a hooker. So it's like nothing is working really. She's in production mode and I'm just giggling and laughing. And at some point one of says stop, I probably say stop. I just can't do this. So we stop and I put my clothes back on and we head out of the bookstore. And I'm still happy, giddy, just can't believe it and so I'm going to go get another drink and I yell at her as she's getting on her bike, "You want to get a beer?" And she says, "No, no thanks" and is already pedaling away. So using the words I know now, I see that I was wanting connection. Wanting to connect with this person regardless of what happened. You know, do you want to sit down and have a beer with me?

Being 18 or 19 and cashing my tax return check was a pretty big deal to me. I went to San Francisco with a whole 225 dollars in my pocket. I'm living life! So I get to the bar and I open my wallet to get a drink and there's no cash in there. And I realized that while she was telling me she's keeping my pants up, she emptied my wallet. She put her fingers in there and took the cash out, and left the wallet. It's amazing I was so gullible. So that was my experience. I was so in that mood, I couldn't really do much. I mean there are a few more details about having a brother who works on the street for a heroin dealer.

I don't remember how I felt after that experience. The ones on the street have never been attractive to me, but I found the sex workers on craigslist attractive. Before the police shut it down, there was an adult section and there were a lot of prostitutes on there. And there were concerned about sex trafficking and all of that. Women say things like, I'd appreciate 250 roses for your visit. Or, I'm looking for a mature man. Now, that kind of entertained me, and of course it's nice to look at with the photos. That would be something I'd more go for. I almost got a job one time for an escort service in Phoenix, and that was interesting. I also almost got a job at a strip bar, but as the driver I would have been the safety for the girl. I'd wait in the parking lot and make sure she gets in and out okay and doesn't get beat up. So something like that, the whole idea was really exciting to me. I want basically an attractive prostitute. So yeah, it's really important that I be physically attracted to them.

You know, I was kind of one in the same way that women are one. I kept a sexual affair going because the woman was giving me money. And I know that played a part in me staying in the relationship. She was giving me money for my custody case, and at the time I would have sold my soul to give the lawyers enough money to get my son back. I mean I really would. So it was pretty easy, I mean she put about 40,000 into my case. I also ended up sleeping with my brother's girlfriend, that's actually where I lost my virginity, and she ended up being a prostitute, but not when I was with her. It was five or six or seven years later, she showed up in Phoenix and me and my friend hung out with her a little bit and she had some good weed, but she had a black eye and some injuries, and now I know it wasn't from the car accident she said. I mean I don't think it was, I think it was because she got hit in her job, or because someone had fun with that as a part of their erotic fantasy or whatever. When I said, "What do you do?" she said, "I deliver packages, very expensive packages." But either I just figured it out or somebody told me. My brother was always in prison and I used to visit him through the glass in different prisons and I think he told me and complained about me having sex with her. I was probably 15 when I lost my virginity to her so I'm not really excited about the story that I lost my virginity to her.

There's a little side story of my brother thinking he's a gangster and putting word out on the street to find this woman and get my money back. He believed there was honesty amongst crooks. And there's a little bit more to the story that I shouldn't have told her in that giddy state. When she said, "What are you doing here?" and I told her I was staying down the street with my brother who sold heroin. And then my brother got busted a couple days later and I feel really confident that that got her a point with the police and she shared that.

So out of this deal of being with a sex worker, I got held at gun point. I was up in the room when the police came in. This cop was your typical undercover drug guy, he had the beard and the earring. You know we're in this room the size of a hotel room and this giant gun comes in. We're all sitting there with our hands up in the air. Yes, it was very scary. Another guy who buys drugs calls on the phone while we're there and the cops tell him to come up and they arrested him too. A year later in prison my brother said, "Be careful who you talk to next time." My brother didn't take revenge or anything, because he just said I was a kid in San Francisco and told the cops where the heroin was so they would let me go. I don't know if my brother is still living. He's 10 or 15 years older than me and I kind of lost track of him. I got into AA and I saw one of my siblings in 2003 at my dad's funeral, but they both have Hep C and they're both addicts and living on the streets. I've been there, living on the street. I lived on the streets a lot too.

Sean

Hollywood, 1982

I had my first experience when I was fourteen, before I'd
even kissed a girl. My sister had a piano recital in San Francisco
which my mom was going to accompany her to. So it was one of
the first weekends ever I was left home alone. So I just reassured
my mom, "I'm going to fine. I'm going to fine," thinking the
whole time, "As soon as they leave, I'm going to call my buddies
and we're going to go joy riding. Because, you know, I have the
keys to the car." So they take off and I call my best friends, we
were like a threesome, and my friend Josh picks up the phone and
I say, "We got the car." Josh had an older brother, so he had
experience driving. We grew up in a suburb outside the city so it
was just residential, there's no action or excitement. I mean the
biggest thing would be going to the shopping mall to go cruising.
It was that kind of thing. So they ride their bikes over and we're
like,

"Where should we go?" and Josh says,

"Hollywood."

So we're 14 growing up in a suburban, picket-fence type
neighborhood and I'd never been into Hollywood at night. And
Hollywood was like, going into the city, and I was a little
nervous, because, what if something happens to the car? But I
okay it because they're so excited and I know there's nothing I can
say to prevent us going to Hollywood now. So we get to
Hollywood and we're just cruising, I don't know, Sunset
Boulevard. Then Josh says, "Where are all the hookers?" Because

at that point we had been watching tv and knew that in
Hollywood there were hookers somewhere. Then we thought to
go to the center of Hollywood, like Hollywood and Vine. So we
go and there are three young women sitting at a bus stop. So Josh
does a U-turn and pulls up right in front of the bus stop, and non
of us are expecting anything, I mean I was 14 and I'd never even
kissed a girl before. I'd never even had a girlfriend. But I'm in the
passenger seat, Josh pulls up and Brett is in the back. So we pull
up and I role down the window, like nervous because these are
older girls, and one of the three women looks at me and says,

"You guys want a date?" And I was thinking, *Oh my god,
they are real life prostitutes!* And none of us had been with a girl
before and I was frozen because I couldn't believe it. It was like
all of a sudden we were in an alternate universe. So I turn to Josh
and Josh looks out the window and says,

"We'll think about it," and he cruises off. Because we
didn't know what to do. And we're all excited about these real live
prostitutes.

So we gather ourselves together and pull up to the same
bus stop, to the same three women, and I'm sure they were
laughing at us, because I mean, we looked 14. But this time, Josh
says,
"How much?" And I remember them saying 20 dollars for
something. But Josh starts playing the adult negotiator and
making up some story like, "You know we just got off of work
and blah, blah, blah." And obviously they could see right through
it. So we drove off, and then there was another corner somewhere,
and as soon as Josh pulls up, two women jump in the car. We
barely said anything, and they just let themselves in. So there was
one woman on my lap and another woman in the backseat. And
the woman on my lap is starting to arouse me through my pants
and saying,

"Oh, look at what we have here." So I, of course, I don't
know what to do, because I've never been with a woman before,

and so I'm not doing anything, but she's sitting there feeling me up through my pants and getting me erect. Which is clever on her part. And unbeknownst to me she is also digging through my pockets and taking my money, which I didn't figure out until we'd driven off. The woman in the back is arousing Brett so much he needed to do something about it, but he had no money. So the woman in the backseat had gotten Brett into a hysteric state. I mean, up until that point, Brett had just been beating off to Playboys. So Brett is saying to Josh,

"Josh, can you lend me 40 bucks?" But Josh is feeling left out because he's got no woman, and he's like,

"Aw man, 40 bucks, you don't have 40 bucks."

"I'll give you my stereo," he says. So Brett gets a blow job in the back seat. And I'm sitting in the front not wanting to impinge on his experience, but I've never seen that happen before. I was peeking over, but I didn't want to look at his crotch. And meanwhile this woman on my lap is trying to negotiate some deal with me, but I wasn't about to do anything. I didn't even know what I wanted. I was still somewhat in shock mode, you know, that this was actually happening. I think the other part of it was – I don't think it was guilt or judgment, but up until that point it was my mom and my older sister who were in the house with me, but I think I just didn't know if it was the right thing to do.

So the woman in the back finishes up with Brett and they popped out of the car and were gone, and Josh and I turn around and are like, "What was that like?" And Brett was telling us and just had a huge smile on his face the whole way home.

"I love my stereo, but it was worth it." he said. And by that time I checked my pockets where I had two twenties and they were gone. And sure enough, we get home and the engine starts steaming, because it turns out there was no oil in the car, and the next morning the car won't start. And we had all shook hands that if anything happened to the car, we would all pay for it. So I had to tell my mom what we did. And it was huge drama and it cost like 600 bucks to fix the engine And my mom felt it was the responsible thing to tell Josh and Brett's parents. So she calls Josh's mom, and being a pastor, she had all this guilt about her son going to Hollywood and messing around with prostitutes. Because I told my mom we met prostitutes, but I didn't tell her that Brett had actually received services, or that I had got robbed. But when she called Josh's mom, she knew everything and just put this whole guilt thing on my mom. My mom was mostly upset about the breach of trust, whereas with Josh's mom, being a pastor, it was more about the prostitutes and sin, and this kind of thing.

So fast forward twenty years later and I'm in Korea on business. And there are these things they call Room Salons. There are a whole variety of them and sometimes business is done in these Room Salons. So essentially you buy the room, and a bottle of Johnnie Walker is like, 1000 dollars, there's a karaoke machine, and these hostesses come out and pour drinks for you and laugh at your stupid jokes, that kind of a thing. So a lot of the salons are on the first floor of hotels, and I didn't know this at the beginning, but you can actually pay for a room to take a hostess to. So these guys I was doing business with, they had paid for our hostess to go to a private room with me. So at the end of the night it was like a surprise, "Here! It's from all of us."

"Guys, you don't need to."

"It's already done," they say, "We've already paid for it." And there's something in Korean culture, where I'm sure in a lot of cultures, where you don't want to reject a gift. Especially since there was so much camaraderie. So I didn't want it, but at the same time, she's adorable, but I'm not sure what's going to happen here, because I've never been in that situation before. So we're going up the elevator. And I'm just not sure what's going to happen here. One, I'm concerned about my health. I mean, I don't know whether these women are tested or not, and beyond that, I'm like, well, what's the right thing to do here? There was just something in me that felt like, she was there to do a job, and for me, so much of the turn on comes from a woman's authentic desire, and it just didn't feel like the right thing.

So we go in and she says, "Shower?" And I think she must want me to be clean. And I'm inebriated, because we've been drinking Johnnie Walker, and I go into the bathroom and there's a basket of condoms next to the sink. So I'm in the shower and I'm thinking, "What the fuck am I going to do? What's the thing to do here?" So I'm half drunk and I come out of the shower and she's naked, and I look away. Then I ask her to lay on her front side. So she lies on the bed and I've got my boxers on and I just started giving her a massage. So I massaged her shoulders and back for about a half an hour and we just talked. I asked her where she was from, and she was from some small town in the countryside, and I asked her how long she had been in Seoul. And by then it was 1:30 in the morning, and I sent her home. And she was really happy.

So then I took a cab back to my friend's place, and to the friends who had all treated me to this 'present', and he said, "How was it?"

"It was fantastic," I said. And that was it.

Ken

Orange County, 1999

Well the only type of person I've ever seen would be a
dominatrix. The first time that I saw one I was probably about 30,
about 18 years ago. Well back then the Internet existed, but it
wasn't what it is today. So basically it was primarily paper based.
There would be a couple of publications where people would
have that, and that's pretty much where you would do your
research. There was an online site that had ads as well. I spent a
lot of time researching before I called somebody because it took a
lot of time before I had the nerve to do it really. And I wanted to
see the right person and I wasn't even sure what I wanted, I just
knew I wanted something I wasn't getting in my personal life.
That I felt like I could only find through a professional. Now you
can just Google people and they have websites with all the stuff
they do, but back then it was more just a one page ad and you had
to kind of base things more on appearance and the ways they
presented themselves, and then you would call them and talk to
them a little bit to get a better idea of what their interests were in
the scene, and if that sounded like any match with you.

But with the first person they were the fantasies I had in
my head and making it a reality. I talked to a couple of people
before I finally booked with somebody. So the first person I
called was someone who actually came to my apartment and it
turned out to be way more of an escort than a dominatrix and it
wasn't a great experience, it wasn't a horrible experience, but I
just knew it wasn't what I was looking for. It was more of a let
down really. Back then I was really just looking for a spanking-
type thing, or light bondage or something. But that was primarily
because that's all I really knew existed. I didn't even know all this

more extreme stuff was out there. I was more looking for the role-play side of things and just trying to figure out what that itch was that I'd always had in my mind, and what it would feel like to make it a reality and not just a fantasy. I probably paid $125 or something for an hour. So she tied my hands and there was some very light spanking, and that was about it. And then she suggested that I pleasure myself in front of her. And I tried, but I couldn't. It just wasn't what I wanted.

After that I just felt like, well that was not what I was looking for. And I kind of knew I had just not made the right choice. It was probably about six months before I sought someone else. The second time was a pretty similar result. It still wasn't what I was looking for. I could tell it wasn't her thing. I mean these women were doing it because it was an aspect of what they chose to do. But they definitely weren't getting anything out of it on their end. After that second one it was a couple years before I saw anyone else. And by then the Internet was the primary source of finding somebody, so I was able to do more detailed research of who might be a better fit. And after a few months I found somebody who was actually a full-time professional Dominatrix who was in downtown LA. So I called her and set up a session and that person ended up being exactly what I was looking for.

I had a girlfriend that I was living with at the time. I had been with her from a really young age, like 18, so at that point we'd been together for 14 years, and when I was 18 although this was a little bit in my mind, it wasn't strong enough to bring it into my personal life. It wasn't until later that it became that way and by that time our relationship was kind of defined and I just didn't feel like it would go over well. And it felt like it would be introducing something that could be incredibly problematic. And at the time I just wasn't comfortable doing it. In retrospect, I probably should of, but I didn't. I think early on when I was first figuring out how to deal with this urge when it comes to kink, I didn't fully understand it, and I had to experience it to come to terms with where it belongs in my psyche, I guess, or my life. Or a place I could find and be comfortable with it. It just seemed like something completely foreign that I just didn't have a great understanding about, so to introduce it to somebody else in my life without having a grasp of it seemed incredibly risky. And at the time I really wouldn't have been able to explain it. Risky in the sense that it could have really damage the relationship, or her view of who we were or who I was. So I guess at the time, because I didn't understand it, there was some guilt or shame about it.

From the very first meeting with the real professional, like half-way through that session I realized that this is exactly what it's always been in my mind, and the fantasy could translate into the real experience and I could get what I thought was actually out there. And it was probably in the first year and a half of seeing her, I would see her about once a month, and that's where I was introduced to all these different aspects of the kink scene that I had had no knowledge about. I had just never considered that it would be part of what I was interested in, but she kind of took me on this journey to try to figure out what exactly I would respond to. Which ended up being very different than what I had had in my head all those years. It ended up being much broader.

Along the way of that first year and a half, it really didn't have much affect on my personal life, it wasn't something I was distracted by or obsessed with or anything. It sort of became compartmentalized in a corner that I would visit every month or so for two hours and then it would just sort of find it's place. And it really didn't interrupt my relationship in any way at the time. We actually ended up getting married a few years later.

The term sex worker within the kink scene was something I only started hearing years ago. From my experience it was never a blatantly sexual thing for me. It was way more mental, I guess. I was sort of going after and finding it, but that was just my experience. The first time I saw the professional player she did order me to do that and I followed instructions, but she could tell halfway through that it was not something I came in for, so she stopped me and we never did that again. It's not that it's not some kind of stimulating turn on in a mental way, it's just not the level that it is. But I would masturbate thinking about it after. It didn't have really any effect on the sex life with my partner turned wife. I mean our sex life was pretty average, it wasn't great, it wasn't horrible.

Along my journey of experiencing all the different aspects of the scene, strap-on play was introduced, but I didn't particularly take to it all that fondly. But it is something I did engage in a couple of times within a scene, but it never ended in ejaculation or masturbation or anything like that, it was used more about a power exchange element, and less as a sexual element. Over the years, my play has changed. At that time, what I discovered that I was most responsive to was a little bit of a power exchange, for sure, but ultimately it became more sensation play or sensory play, which includes being blindfolded and having all kinds of things that I didn't know what they were happen to me that I would feel on a really high level. And sometimes that would include great pain, and sometimes things that felt incredibly good. And because it was completely blindfolded, it would allow me to escape for that period of time, which I was never able to do in my day to day life. Pain is an element. At that time pain was not a big draw for me, though it wasn't a hard limit, and it was certainly included, because it's pretty much included at some level in all S&M play, but at that time I wouldn't have considered myself in any way a masochist. But it could be needle play, hot wax, burning ointment, or things that felt good, but I don't even know what most of the things were, I just know what they felt like.

So I don't go anymore at all. I actually ultimately ended up in a couple and living with that Dominatrix that I met 18 years ago. Which only developed a year ago, so there was a long relationship between as client and friend. With me and her, on a client-professional level I always felt incredibly close to her, but it wasn't ever a sexual intimacy that I felt, just a really unique singular connection, and over the years it would be huge breaks like six months or a year, just depending on where I was at in my life. So we wouldn't see each other monthly or that consistently over all those years. And so our relationship for the first probably ten years, we enjoyed talking before and after as a friend level, but we didn't have any connection with each other outside those sessions. And then she retired from the scene when she had children and was gone for about five years, and then when she came back I started seeing her again and it was about within a year of that that our relationship just somehow naturally progressed into something else.

We had about a six-month affair and then I left my wife. Of course I didn't tell her that it was a Dominatrix I had been seeing off and on for 18 years, but she just knew that there was another woman. She had found during the six months she had found a couple of things that clued her into that there was a kink element, not that there would be any reason to believe there was a professional Dominatrix involved. But she had found some things that brought my kink to life.

So it wasn't clear exactly how our relationship and the kink would meld initially, so it was sort of something we had to figure out along the way. Initially when we first got together, it was no different than any other relationship. I definitely would call it more or less vanilla early on. As the affair progressed, we continued to occasionally play and we kept it a little bit separate. And we would play with each other in the space of a studio or dungeon. But we figured out pretty quickly that that wasn't going to work anymore because of our relationship. Our minds just didn't, it just wasn't connecting the way it did before. So our kink overtime has become intertwined in everything in our relationship. The sex is, we do have just regular sex often, and sometimes it will be, I wouldn't say role-play, but it will be kind-involved. It's probably 50-50 when that happens, it's not planned, it just turns into something, whether it be tying up somebody's hands, or slapping somebody- it could be anything really. For us, everything is on the table at any time, on both sides. We actually switch back and forth, though she's predominately the dominant one.

It is weird because for most of my adult life I've had this corner that I've kept more or less hidden from everyone in my life, with the exception of a couple of close friends, and now it is, I mean there is still family and stuff, and it's not something we bring up, but for the most part it's not something hidden at all. And it's absolutely incredible. It's like a weight that's not there anymore. It feels pretty good. And especially being in a relationship with someone I'm not hiding anything from. So that has also made for a much healthier relationship. I have one son and she has two daughters from our previous marriages, and our kids are with us 50 percent of the time. I'm 48 now. I think I will probably marry her. It's something that, I mean we could not get married, it really wouldn't marry like when I was younger and it just felt like something that you do. For us I think that we are so confident having had other long term relationships that we have found what both of us always wanted that it just seems like marriage would be something we would offer each other as really just a gesture of the commitment really. The marriage part is just to show others maybe. We've both talked about it and its something we both seem to want, and why that it is, I don't know, it just feels like the right thing. I'm confident that this is it. There will be no one else for me. And marriage just seems like the way to cement that idea.

Sam

Los Angeles, 2010

Well the first time I had her come to me. I found her on
Backpages.com, which is like a seedier version of Craigslist. I've
never had penetrative sex with a sex worker. I just could never
imagine myself doing it. I thought there was a whole world of risk
with that and it just seemed too far outside my range. Like, what
if she's a cop and I'm being entrapped? Everything from that to,
well what if she's got some STD? Even a condom is not enough
protection. I don't know, it's just my mind went there. But I just
had this idea that I needed to try something different from the
masturbating.

So for a long time I would just go on Backpages and look
at the ads and sometimes I couldn't tell if they were for sex or not.
I found this woman that seemed really young, probably looked
twenty or twenty-one and what's going through my mind was, *Is
this really her?* I think I called her. The whole thing was not
super fulfilling. Plus I'm pretty frugal so it's like, *Why am I
spending money on this?* But each experience was unique. This
first woman was young. So we talked on the phone and she came
to my place. I remember thinking she was really slender, young-
looking, kind of waif-like, and I was like, *Okay this is great.* She
was coming to give me a massage with a happy ending – at least I
was pretty sure that was on the menu. So I figured I'd try it out
and worst case scenario I get a massage. And as it turns out, every
time I try it, it's just a lousy massage, and a rushed kind of hand
job. There was another ad with her picture that seemed like she
did have sex with her clients, johns, whatever you call them, but
she seemed afraid.

I think I asked her, "Do you want to use the massage table?" She was surprised I had a massage table. She was probably used to doing it in the bedroom. So I started face down and it was just this rudimentary massage all over the place, and I was kind of disappointed. I think she was topless but not bottomless. It was not as mentally stimulating as I hoped it would be. Like I said, she seemed scared or uncertain about herself. So then I flipped over and I don't know, but her lack of confidence that was a turn off and a turn on at the same time. I don't know if she was wanting me to be more aggressive and tell her what I wanted, but eventually she did some massage in the front and then she had some kind of slippery lubrication she rubbed on my penis. She didn't say anything. It was really just the slippery stuff on her hands that felt really good. I was very disappointed. One thing I thought was strange was that the girl wasn't even pretending to be into it. I felt like I got a quasi-expert or something. Yes, I came after a while, but I think it was more because I was visually stimulated by what she looked like. She was young and slender, and yeah, she was topless.

In each of the experiences I didn't know if I could touch the woman or not. It sensed the first one was not comfortable with that. So it was just okay. And at this point I was asking myself, *Do I do this again? What was the point?* It was satisfying, but not fulfilling, but it was an interesting experience. You know, I could check that one off the list. I think at that point I was really just feeling lonely in my life and I wanted some physical touch. I didn't just want to get a massage, but like I said, I was too afraid of the risks involved to actually have a prostitute or someone who's going to do the full menu, so to speak.

So I found this ad with another girl who did "massage" and I forgot what exactly her ad said. But she came over, and she was much more free with her body and definitely naked. She was nervous and afraid like the first one though – it's so weird I attracted women like that! So she started giving me a massage and she asked me what I did, and when I told her I was a massage therapist she was like,

"Oh, maybe you can teach me!" So she gave me a massage and I was giving her some suggestions. Then I turned over and she gave me a hand job and it felt good and I came. We left it that she would come back and I would teach her some massage and she would practice on me. Which I was thinking, *Well great, that's free!* She was not a pro in trying to make money from this and she would talk about the other men she saw. She told me she was just trying to make a little extra cash, and I asked her if she ever slept with any of her clients, and she said,

"Once, because I liked the guy."

Anyway, when she came over again, this time I got a little more adventurous in touching her. I could tell she had desire and fear at the same time. I was touching her and I could feel that her pussy was wet and she was aroused, but she didn't want me to touch her. It was really interesting to me that she kind of got to this point where she was not wanting to be touched. But then when I massaged her she really enjoyed it. It was nice to actually elevate her massage and actually get a bit of a massage too. I think we only did a trade a total of three times. And I was actually just as excited about touching her as being touched. I wanted to touch her pussy and feel her desire for that and her wetness and arousal. But her fear was a turn off. It didn't feel hot. It wasn't like I was looking to be dominated or led so much as I wanted to feel a woman who was into it. Someone who was turned on and enjoying the experience of doing what she was doing.

My next experience was so different. First of all, she was not the girl from the pictures, and I remember she had this wacky story that she wanted to be on Playboy and that was her life goal or something like that. She was a little bit chubby, but if she lost a little weight I'm sure she could have been in Playboy. I thought she was pretty. But she definitely knew how to up-sell. I mean from the minute she walked in the door it was like, "If I take my clothes off it's this much more, and if I touch you, it's this, or I can use a vibrator on myself, and it's that," but clearly there was no sex on the menu. Though later I wondered if I had offered enough money that it might have been on the menu. Oh, and she stole one of my bath towels – a hand towel. She went into the bathroom and got ready and came out in panties and we chose to do the massage in the bedroom and she started out giving me a massage and at some point she took her panties off and got out the vibrator. I thought it was really hot to watch her masturbate. I think she squirted but not profusely, but it was hot to see her have a climax. I was masturbating at the same time. She was at my side and she was close, and I think she let me touch her breasts a little bit, and one of the things that really excited me was that she was aroused by me stroking my cock. She was clearly turned on by that. And I remember I just really wanted to go down on her. But I never said anything and she came and I came and then she left and stole my towel.

So the last one was the most unique experience of all. I found some site and there were these women who were Tantrikas, and it described in real detail what to expect. It was not sex, but it was a completely sensual massage. The woman would be nude, and it was likely at the end she would give me a hand job, or what in Tantra they call a lingam massage. So when I arrived at her home there was incense burning – it was an experience. What made it really great was that this was someone who was really invested in what she was doing. She enjoyed it and felt like she was being of service somehow. And it felt good to walk into that environment. So this was the only time I ever went to somebody, and I walked in and she was this petite, tiny little body – totally my type – and she gave me a hug. She might have been topless, but it was so cool to be embraced when I walked in the door. It felt like I was being welcomed into her space. And it was sensual and soothing in an interesting way. It was what I wanted in a lover. I wanted to feel like I was met, like that sense of push back. I didn't want someone dominant or submissive, I wanted to feel that sense of connection. Maybe there was that back and forth of someone leading and someone following, but I wanted that connection that was unique. So when she hugged me when I walked in the door, that's what I walked into.

I wasn't sure if she was the same person on the website, but I didn't care, because it felt good. She had me take a shower, so that was cool, and felt like part of the experience. She had the massage table set up and the most hysterical thing was that it was the most uncomfortable massage table I had ever been on. So I was face down, and I'm pretty sure she was completely nude and I was too, and I think the room was pretty warm and she was using warmed coconut oil. She used her entire body throughout the experience and both her hands and it was so sensual. It was almost like it wasn't sexual though, like it was a treatment. I don't think I ever get aroused during a normal massage. And this felt super, super sensual but it didn't quite cross over into sexual. So I was like semi-erect for pretty much all of it, but never wanting to devour her. Most of the massage was face down, but I was so impressed that she was doing this dance – like this was an artist – so different from the other experiences. This woman was into what she was doing, like it was an art form for her. So I felt like I was being honored. Then I turned over and she straddled me and did some more of the massage, but still it was in that zone of sensuality that was soothing and nourishing, but there was something that never crossed over into the sexual. Again that went on for a long time and she was just taking her time, and I didn't feel like she was rushing it. She was engaged and I felt her intention and attention. Then she straddled my legs and for the first time she gave my cock her full attention and she was stroking gently and slowly, and I could feel her full attention on me. It was so interesting that it was nourishing and soothing and arousing, and I was hard the whole time, but I never reached a peak and I'm not sure why. At a certain point I thought she was getting annoyed thinking this is taking a long time. And then it got to this point where I could feel her body getting impatient, as she had sped up and was intensifying the sensation. It was like I got the message in my brain that she wanted me to come already but I couldn't come. She was petite and sexy and I don't know why it was I couldn't come. It was almost like her intention switched to trying to get me off and I felt like I was left there. So she started to slow down, and she covered me with a towel, put pressure on my cock, and said, "You get to keep your seed."

What was interesting was that leading up to that experience I had been reading about Tantra and withholding ejaculation and I just found it really fascinating that it was so different than the other experiences. I showered again because I was drenched in coconut oil. It was so interesting was that it was nourishing but not sexual. She was pretty expensive too, close to $300. The other one who up-sold me was pretty much the same. I guess I felt overall underwhelmed by the experiences. Besides my conditioned feeling that this was bad or elicit behavior, it wasn't as rewarding as I'd hoped. It wasn't a match for my financial investment either. I wanted to feel connected and to have a heart connection because I probably felt more lonely during that period of my life than I had felt in a long, long time. I didn't have any lovers at the time. I think it was right after my mom passed away. I thought that having a sexual connection with someone might do something for me but it didn't.

So it was just underwhelming and disappointing. And what's so interesting is when I've been in Amsterdam – and you know, it's legal there and the prostitutes are checked – I never really found anyone I was attracted to. I must have been on the wrong streets or something. Except once, I was walking to dinner with some friends and I looked over into this window in an apartment under the stairs there was this gorgeous young woman. I felt like telling my friends,

"I'll meet up with you in a few minutes!" But I didn't and it's so interesting because I have friends who have told me they've gone to Amsterdam and been with prostitutes, but it always seemed like too great a health risk to me. But I'm sure more than anything, it's just my conditioning that it's bad.

Gerry

Amsterdam, 2013

I was in Amsterdam and I was like, *I'll never hire a hooker but I want to have the experience once, at least.* And I wanted to have it in Amsterdam because that's the *crème de la crème,* and I don't need hookers at home. I don't need to pay someone for sex so I only want to do that in Amsterdam. So I went and I was walking around the red light district and I saw a lot of girls in windows, but t,here was this Russian chick with a black chick, and the Russian chick was dancing and I thought it was sexy, so I went in and she's like,

"You want both of us?" And I was like,

"How much? Fifty for both?" And she's like,

"No $100, $50 for one." I said,

"Alright, I just want you." So I went with the Russian chick and I'm undressing and whatever because she's like

"Ooh, yeah, take all your clothes off," and when that was done she said, "Lay down." So I lay down and it's almost like a medical cot or something and she puts this little square paper towel with a dick hole in it over my dick and then she puts the condom on but the way she did it was really mechanical like she's done it one hundred times a day for the past ten years or something. She's just so mechanical about it.

So I did a little research before I went in and apparently

you have to make them agree to the whole thing, like anything
you want, you want to touch them at all, you have to agree to that
before you give them money. So I gave her a very stern suck-and-
fuck- fifty euros, and she agreed, whatever. So, you know, she's
sucking me dick or whatever, with the condom on it – they're
very safe – and then she's like,

"Your dick is too big. I might have to charge you another
fifty euros" and I'm just like,

"You know, we had an agreement: suck and fuck- fifty
euro. You're going to fuck." She said,

"We'll see," and she kept going down on me, and she was
really good but nobody's ever made me come giving head, so
especially with a condom on, there's no way. But she was trying,
because they're done with they get you off. If you take too long,
it's a problem. But the point is they get kind of impatient because
they want to make their next client so she was like, "Alright, we'll
fuck." And it was really cold out so my hands were freezing and I
kept putting them around her waist and she wasn't into it because
we didn't agree to it before I gave her money. I was behind her
and she was up on a chair. She was naked, totally fake boobs,
Russian, barely spoke English, just enough to hustle me. The
point is she kept trying to get more money out of me and I was
like,

"No, I don't have any more money, but you're going to
give me what I paid for." She kind of turned me off since she was
hustling me, and she was saying, "Yeah, baby," and "Your cock's
too big," but they say that to everyone.

So she got irritated with me with the whole cold hands
thing and so she was like, "I'll finish you off," so she just gave me
a hand job and then I left. But the point is, afterwards, I was
getting dressed, and she was like douching herself or something at
the sink whatever and she's like,

"Get out," totally rushing me to get dressed, and I'm like,

"It's freezing. I've got layers." It was weird leaving there. It was almost like I didn't have sex with somebody. There's like no connection. It's an extremely physical, purely physical release and no emotion at all. I didn't really care for it. It's not even that sexy to think back on. Like I wouldn't masturbate thinking about it. I get off on passion and connection and that's just not what it was. Would I have said yes to the two girls if I'd had infinite funds? No, I'm Jewish. Would I do it again? I don't know, I'm not completely closed to it. It wasn't a horrible experience, but probably not. Like, I wouldn't be upset if I never did it again. But like if one day I find myself in Amsterdam or something again and I feel like doing it, you know, I might do it. But probably, more than likely not.

Brice

East Hollywood, 2002

I'd been in LA for five or six years, and was single at the time. I'd just gotten out of a relationship and was working long hours, was super busy at work and didn't have much time for dating. I was trying dating sites, but didn't have the time/energy for it, and I was still recovering from the break up, and not really looking for anything serious. There's this whole world online, it's inundated. I definitely had a type I was looking for. I wanted someone older, like late twenties (I was in my early to mid-thirties at the time) with real body parts and someone who sounded articulate. Their pictures really mattered. Something artistic in their pictures would grab my eye. I had a really good income, so the money wasn't an issue, so I used that as a filter to look for higher end escorts.

I found one and we communicated back and forth for a bit and she suggested we meet at a bar/restaurant first. I lived in the East Hollywood Hills area near Los Feliz, so I recommended an artsy little bar in the area and she knew it and I thought that was cool. When I saw her, based on her appearance, she was someone I would totally want to date. She showed up in business attire, very conservative. She had her Masters degree and was getting her Ph.D. We started talking and she was super articulate and friendly and we had some drinks and went back to my place. We spent two hours together. It cost close to $1000 per hour. The sex happened really quickly and easily. I remember that it was a really cool experience. It was like an awesome date with real authentic feelings. It made me think, *Wow, I wish I could meet someone like this outside of sex work.*

I saw her at least two more times after that, and the second to last time we went to a swingers club, very high-end, with masks and all. The night of the party she stayed over and let me pay by check, and she gave me her real name. We had to write on the check that it was for interior design. She didn't charge me for the hours we were sleeping. She had just started into the business a couple of months before. I liked paying with a check better than cash because it meant that she trusted me with her real name. It also wasn't so transactional that time because it wasn't for every hour. She really enjoyed the party and we drove in her car because it was nicer than mine at the time.

I had to been to parties before in LA that were okay, but this one was the best. It was very high-end and felt very exclusive. There were very attractive people there, not trashy porny. It was in a huge mansion in the Hills. I'd been in LA for a while and was pretty open sexually and had experienced a lot. I was kind of open to everything. We went to a room when we got there and had vaginal and oral sex and when I looked up I realized that people were watching us. She played with some women at the party too. We made some clear rules before we went, so we knew what to expect. It was funny because people were coming up to us and saying,

"You are such a cute couple." But I didn't want it to be a more permanent thing, and ended up dating someone a normal way after that.

A couple of years later I found myself single and I hired a sex worker again and it was not a good experience. It made me realize I had lucked out the first time. The person wasn't as attractive to me in-person, wasn't as articulate, and didn't have the conservative dress. This time she came to my place, we made small talk, drank some wine, and then we had sex. It felt very artificial. I found her attractive, but we had nothing in common. And I didn't do it again for years. And I questioned whether her orgasms were real. It all just felt like it lacked authenticity.

I had a rule that I wouldn't do it if I was dating somebody. But years later I was starting to date someone, and I did it again in San Francisco. Her name was Julia. She just came to my place, we had drinks and talked about experiences and traveling and we discovered we were both skiers, so that was cool. She was a huge traveler and she worked as an escort to get money to travel. This experience felt more like the first time. We had a great connection and we had oral, vaginal and anal sex. I saw her one more time after that and she brought a friend to have a threesome, but it wasn't as good. I wasn't as attracted to her friend. I was also still dating another person and I felt guilty, like I was hiding something. The times I did it before it would fill the gap between girlfriends, but I didn't like the feeling of doing it when I was dating someone. It skewed the perception of the person I was dating. It was unfair. It's not like I felt like I was going to fall in love with the person I was dating, but I remember thinking, *Don't do that again.* That baggage affected the experience. It wasn't as cool.

After the threesome, Julia was traveling and not around, and I assumed she ended up not doing that work anymore because her website went down. It was pretty shortly after that I saw someone whom I ended up getting married to and then separated from. After the separation I didn't really want to date anyone, so it made me look at the escort thing again. San Francisco didn't really have what I was looking for and I was renting my house in Venice and going there a lot and that's where I saw Kendra's ad. I was staying at a friend's house and I invited her over. She walked in and was blonde (brunettes are my type) but she also had this amazing body and she started talking and the connection was there really quickly. She turned out to be awesome and we've seen each other three or four times since then. That first time we walked to the store and got some wine, and it was suppose to be an hour and a half, but it was a lot longer. I initiate the touching. We talked a lot and then had great sex- oral and vaginal, but mostly anal. And I felt really connected because that takes a level of trust. The problem is she's in LA and I'm in San Francisco, and it feels a little bit weird to say, "Hey I'm dating someone, but if

I'm not dating someone, can we meet up?" $1400/hour. $2600 for two.

What I'm doing is a total secret, even from my twin brother. He's been married for ten years. I don't think he'd judge me, but I think he'd be more like, "Holy shit, you have that much money to throw away?" I think he would think it's a waste of money. He's has some strip club experiences, but he thinks it's very transactional. I paid the last one $1400 per hour, or $2600 for two. It feels good in the moment but then you think, *I wasted a ton of money.*

If I don't get married again, I think I've become more comfortable with it being a stopgap. If I'm single and I want that sexual energy and experience, I have the money to do it. I could foresee myself doing it more. I've definitely gotten more comfortable with it over time. And really, four women in 15 years is not that many.

Steven

Seattle, 2015

I'm not in-between relationships. I'm married, quite happily, but my wife and I have different ideas about sex, the frequency, positions, oral versus vaginal versus anal, etc.. I really enjoy sex and she enjoys it some, but she doesn't like to give or receive oral, and we don't have sex as often as I'd like. She's quite happy with the amount that we do have sex. We had this conversation and at one point she said,

"You can go have a girlfriend, just don't ever introduce me to her because I'll tear her apart." And so, I don't really want a girlfriend, but I do want to enjoy the girlfriend experience, so to speak. I loved, when I was dating, I loved dating. I love finding out about people, getting to know them – and so I just decided that escorts would be a better way to go than finding a girlfriend.

So I've been seeing escorts for about two years. I'm extremely active. I see probably two escorts a week. Some are ones that I see frequently and others are new people I see on business. I travel a lot for my job. For example I'm doing an overnight tonight, an overnight tomorrow night with someone else who's traveling to meet me where I am, and then she and I are traveling back to my home city and meeting up with another escort and doing a double overnight, so three nights in a row. Last week I flew from Washington DC from California to have a two day overnight with an escort in DC. That was the first time I had met her in person. We had emailed quite a lot and had tried to meet up earlier in Toronto because I was going to be there for business, but it didn't work out, so we basically emailed for a couple of months. The emails are mostly getting to know each other. Sometimes they get a little sexy, but not usually. They're logistics like, should we get a suite with a nice big tub for the two of us, or downtown as suppose to near some kind of venue, those types of logistical things. But usually they're not sexy, no, it's more of getting to know the person. I occasionally share my picture, it's just a corporate photo, a generic shot of me standing with my arms crossed looking diagonally, like every corporate website photo.

I meet up with escorts in other cities because I don't have a fear of running into anyone I know there. I don't have a fear of running into anyone in Seattle or Toronto or DC. I live in the South Bay area, and I only know two people in San Francisco proper, but I get concerned about bumping into someone. I have a very close friend who knows, who will take it to his grave and will not share it with anyone. I have another close friend, but doesn't know the level of detail that the other friend knows. And I trust him, but I don't trust him with the same level of details that I trust the other friend. I don't want it to be widely known. It's private. It is something that I really enjoy doing. I don't tell people what I spend on it because I spend an enormous amount of money on it. There's actually one other person who knows about it and that's my physician. I have Parkinson's disease and one of the medications makes you compulsive, if you're prone to compulsivity and I told her because I was wondering if this drug was causing me to participate in this to a greater degree. So we actually backed me off of it. She didn't care. She knows that this happens, and some people gamble or take other kind of adrenaline risks, some people tend to drink, and if they're prone to drinking they drink too much, so we backed my dose way down and nothing really changed. I'm not obsessing about it, but I think about it and I enjoy it. So it wasn't really from the medication. But I had to let her know why I wanted to back off the medication and see if it had any impact. I felt absolutely no judgment from her. Because she knows that people they'll gamble, they'll shop, they'll drink or do drugs, whatever they're prone to this medication can enhance that compulsive behavior.

There's the stigma associated with it. First of all, you're with someone other than your wife. And I see escorts of all ages. Generally I don't go out in public with very, very young, like twenty year olds or twenty-one, more like thirty or forty. I actually see an escort who is my age, in her fifties, I'll be 53 in March. The stigma says, "You're a pervert," "How much sex do you have to have?" I get these types of questions. One of the escorts that I travel with quite a bit, we'll fly together, sit next to each other and check in together and everything. We have a set story of what her name is, she goes by a fake name, but I obviously know her real name because I buy airplane tickets and need to know her real name and we have a whole fake story of why we're together, if anyone were to ask. It's funny because she has a nickname for me, "Cautious adrenaline junkie."

My greatest experience was a trip with the provider who I just mentioned. She and I travel a lot together. We've been to Monterey together, the racetrack, Portland, Seattle a couple of times, Chicago together. I would have to say, the time I spend with her is probably the most genuine time. We were here in Seattle, I'm here now on a business trip. And we just had an incredible dinner, it wasn't a super fancy place, but the conversation, the ambience, the connection, the sex was just great. We were away from San Francisco so I knew I wasn't going to run into anyone I would know. It was just a great experience that we had. The room that I get had this giant two person claw-foot tub and we can sit at opposite ends and just talk. It's the connection that is much more important. I mean the sex is great, and it's part of the reason, but the connection is much more important. Because in my opinion, sex without connection is just too mechanical and boring and it is not why I do it. I generally try to find people I have some type of connection with. I'm not going to do this forever, maybe six or twelve more months. She thinks it's great that I step into this world and step out of this world. It's a secret world that many, many people don't know about it, and what they think they know about it is completely wrong. It was so comfortable and she and I were so connected that we were lying in bed together late, late at night and just instinctively I said, "I love you," and she said, "I love you, too." It's not that I don't love my wife, but I love her as well. And I know nothing is going to happen, and she knows nothing is going to happen, and she's creating a world in her space where she's going to be getting out of the escort world. And I've done things for her that I would not do for others. She lives on a boat and needed a new engine so I bought two new engines for her boat. She didn't ask for that. The other thing was I paid for her to get Lasik eye surgery and I'm going to buy her a truck that she needs. And those types of things allow her to get those things much faster and be able to get out of escorting and start the business that she wants to start. She's not asked for any of it. I've offered it and even when I said, "I'd be happy to pay for your laser surgery," she said, "Well why don't you think about it for a little bit a little longer." So I sat there three, four, five seconds and said, "Okay, I thought about it some more."

I'm probably not going to do this more than six or twelve more months because I don't want to be outed as a client. Not that someone would intentionally do it, but I inadvertently run into someone, or make a mistake and leave my laptop open on the wrong page, something like that. Then I'm done. Also, I'm spending a huge amount of money. I was at a company that got bought by a big company and made a lot of money. That's why I have this disposable income. But I don't want to squander it all away. And I know that what I do is generally not what most clients do. I mean, I always get suites, I always fly everybody first class, I always fly first class myself, and we go to very nice dinners. Tonight we're going out to a restaurant, and the last time we were there, for two of us, the bill was over 400 dollars. But I have that money, and I hate talking about it because I don't want to sound like I'm bragging, but I have it and I want to spend it the way I want to spend it. I worked very hard to get where I am, and you know, got my degrees that I needed to get, and worked hard at various jobs, big companies and small companies, and timing wise, was at the right place at the right time. I was at a particular pharmaceutical company and we got bought and those of us who were there early enough on, made a killing.

What am I going to do when I stop? I don't know. I'm not sure. There's a flaw in my plan. My wife and I have never talked about it again. I've thought of bringing it up to my wife and saying, "What did you mean by that?" But it's been some time and it would seem a little peculiar I think if I were to bring it up. Seeing her and escorts has carried over into my personal life and allowed me to feel much more comfortable talking about sex with my wife, and new positions, and things like that. My wife and I have been married 25 years, and about four months ago was the first time we ever did it doggie-style. Which is, you know, a very common position, and just the other night trying new positions I brought it up afterwards and said,

"Well that was kind of new. That was fun. Kind of a new position," and she said,

"Really?" and I said,

"Yeah, we've never done that before!" She said,

"We haven't?" And I didn't even ask for it. It was a position she just kind of worked her way into.

I am kind of weaning myself off of it too, because of the cost. So what I'm doing is I come to Seattle every month for two nights, so I'll probably do something here. And I want to do something each month with my favorite person, the one whom I'm helping get the business started. And then I do something kind of fun, like meeting someone new in a new city. Like in January I'm meeting someone new in Chicago. What interested me about her was she had a hard science degree and was a college professor for a while. I also have a hard science degree and a Ph.D., and never taught college, but it was a connection and we started talking and she was like, "Oh you skydive? I've always wanted to skydive," or "You race cars? I would love to race cars." I mean our dinner conversation will be effortless because we have so many different things in common. It's that connection kind of thing. There has to be some kind of hook, some kind of connection. Physically I have no type, I see women with real breasts, fake breasts, tall people, short people, skinny, heavier, white, African American, Hispanic- so physically no, what I find is that I will never repeat if there's no connection. And I've met a few I have pretty good connections with, like the woman I met who is my age who is also in the medical, pharmaceutical area. Her "day job" or civilian job is with a company that I could potentially run into with my line of work, so we have a lot of things in common, and we're the same age, so my references from growing up, she get's them. If you're with a twenty-two year old and you make a reference, they're like, "What?" So there has to be some kind of connection, and with the women I do have that connection with, I tend to see them repeatedly. So the woman who is my age, I've seen her 23 times in two years, so I see her almost every month. The woman I travel with, we've seen each other probably 12-14 times in just under a year, and most of those were not a two hour session, they were traveling or for example, like when she came with me down to our beach house and we tore out some tile and took it to the dump. I'm pretty sure there's no escort in the entire city of San Francisco that can say, "Yes, as a part of my date. I went to a landfill," except this one. And she was like,

"I've really never been to a landfill. What's it like?" And I was like,

"Well I'm going to go if you wanna go?" And she said,

"Let's go. Let's get rid of it." So I've done resorts and landfills. On average I pay about $500 an hour. I've paid as much as $7000 for an overnight. I've paid as much as $1000/hour for a three hour session. Three hours is the shortest session I'll do. So mine are almost always overnights or three to six hours.

Who initiates the sex is kind of a combination. Like with one of the woman I see fairly often, the one I'm going to be with tomorrow night, she and I are going to do a duo with another woman the next night. And we've been experimenting with rope tying and bondage and stuff like that, but I'm not that into it. I'm more of a vanilla guy. Threesomes? Well it's hit or miss. I'm lukewarm about them sometimes. I just had a threesome when I was in Washington DC and it was interesting because it was almost overstimulation and I went completely soft and I was like, "What? How can this possibly be?" And then I've had some that were just incredible. I've only had about half a dozen duos. But sometimes it's a little awkward, like does this person kiss that person? What are we going to do? And it's sometimes just a very sexy turn on to see two women enjoying each other.

I wouldn't have a girlfriend on the side because it would feel too much like I'm cheating. Whereas I still sometimes feel like I'm cheating with an escort, but it's a business transaction. Except for certain ones, they don't contact me when I'm not with them. One escort explained it as, the money you pay me is the money to keep me from calling you. Because there's a guarantee that I will never try to get ahold of you. Because otherwise it's not a business relationship anymore. Now, the one I talk with all the time, I told her she can contact me anytime she wants, and I told her how to contact me and we have a little system worked out. And I have that relationship with just one other provider. Yes, when the sex stops the relationship will continue with one of them for sure. If sex were to be in it, I would suspect that it would have to be paid for, because I would be uncomfortable otherwise, but just sharing exciting things happening in each other's lives – my son graduating from college; meeting for lunch and doing something that reminds us of when we first met; milestones in her life; her company doing well; she having a significant other; getting married – those kind of things. I would expect that for the one person that I've talked mostly about. I could see us maintaining some kind of connection for certainly twenty years or the rest of our lives, that type of thing. She's just an incredible person, and although we're twenty years apart, it's so comfortable that it's just great. But it would only be that one. It is a very special relationship and we've talked about it a lot, what the relationship has done for both of us.

Yes, it's a business relationship, and I understand that, she understands that, but it's very, very emotionally connected relationship as well. In fact, she and I were texting two days ago and it was very, very late, I don't even remember how we started texting. It was 1:30 in the morning and she was driving an unfamiliar vehicle, a friend's truck with questionable reliability from somewhere into Oakland and I said to her, "Just text me when you get home safe." Which is what I would do for any friend. I fell asleep, but I woke up in the morning and the last text she sent was, "Safe." And that is a relationship that I don't have with any other provider. She's had a really hard week recently, and we were trying to work some details out for our visit with each other and she said, "Oh, I would love to come along when you go to Seattle because it would be very comforting to spend two nights and a day in Seattle and just hang out and go out to dinner." So from her standpoint, our relationship is a comforting place. Sometimes it's nothing sexual and we'll just lie there with her head on my chest and we'll just chitchat for two hours. She's very intelligent, and I think that's one of the things that attracts me to her the most, to all of the ones I've really enjoyed spending time with. Just like any other profession there are all ranges of intelligence.

The first time she and I came to Seattle we went to a map store. We're both geeks, we both like maps, and we're looking at this map and she starts reading it to me, and I looked at her and said,

"You read Latin?" and she said,

"No, I speak Latin, I used to teach it." I said,

"How did I not know this about you after knowing you for a year?" So she's reading Latin off a map from the 1300s. I tell you this because I think there's a stigma that women do this work because they're dumb and they have no other way to make any money. And that's completely not what I've found. Now there are some women that don't appear to be as intelligent. But there are women that do this that speak Latin. They have sent scientific projects into space that have collected data and they've analyzed the data. There's a whole range. I think that it's a bad stereotype that they're all just floozies. I'm sure you've heard things along those lines. Some of them are leaving graduate school with no debt and a Ph.D. in a hard science or Art History, and some of them are the only people in their family who have gone to college because they paid for it this way. So for them, it's a way to better their situation and I consider it a legitimate business, and feel that it should be legalized and decriminalized in the United States. Because the women I see are not trafficked at all. This is either what they do for a living, it's their business, and its' what they think about all the time, like hair, makeup, background for photo shoots, website design – everything that goes along with running a business- getting clients. If you don't advertise you're just going to sit there and do nothing. They have to learn what works with advertising, and what doesn't and what are clients looking for. What triggers them to send that first message? And the others are people who are doing it to go somewhere else, like get a degree, or earn the money to start a certain business.

There are times when I leave a session and say, "Wow, that was amazing!" And other times where I leave and say, "Wow, I could have used that money for a set of slings for my new race car." Because there's just no connection or sensuality. I like my sessions to be sensual interactions. Like I said, I'm pretty vanilla.

Beau

Tijuana, 1958

Oh my goodness, what sallow part of this world was I in? I was down in Tijuana. What was I? 13 or 14. Oh absolutely nothing happened. We were in Mexico and I thought, well it's time to have some fun. And that's about it, nothing happened. How did I find them? At that time if you sneezed, you'd bump into three of them. Some were in the streets, some were in the bars, I mean they were everywhere. It used to be a wide-open town in the truest sense of wide-open. It wasn't at a bar, cause I was afraid of bars. I requested oral sex. I probably paid about 20 bucks. But the oral sex never happened. I became very frightened of the area I was in, excused myself and went away. And rightfully, it was a dangerous place. No law and order whatsoever. You were on your own. I was going to go to some shady motel and I just wouldn't do it. I may be stupid but I'm not that stupid. I remember I walked a little bit and I just felt terribly uncomfortable. Actually I gave the cab driver the money and that's when I really got nervous. That's as much as I remember. Now understand, this transcript could go in the Smithsonian, I really don't remember the finer details.

Well I'll tell you, I went to boarding school and I attracted a lot of women and there was a woman named Sally, and Sally and I would get it on all the time. To the point where if we went on a school trip they wouldn't let us in the same car. Honestly! So yes, I had a lot of sex- a real hobby! Birth control? Not my problem. Never thought of it. So no need for a sex worker, no. My God, I was tired.

Oh boy. It may have been after I was married. It was not a very productive relationship. And that was in the early seventies. There was nothing there sexually. She was a virgin in every sense of the word. There was just no getting past that. That's the story! I was well aware that my kink side existed, and I was constantly curious, so at one point or another, I dived in. Now the other thing is, clients would come to me with problems related to that business, so I became more and more interested in it, and more and more, I don't know if I was seduced into it, but the offer was constantly there. I practiced a lot of business law, so a lot of my clients did not have problems related to the law, but I would handle them. At the time I was corporate counsel for the biggest 900 number machines, so anyway, everything came past my desk. Every idea, sexual or nonsexual. Everybody had an idea how they were going to make a fortune. They weren't. So I handled the calls and became vice president of the company. But my clients peeked enough interest that I went investigating myself. The funny thing is, at the time, I was a pretty healthy sized guy, and a couple of times people said, "Would you like to be my driver?" Which I guess is like a "bodyguard" but I never did. I feel uncomfortable when I deal with these people, because I can't read them, if you know what I mean.

It was a massage parlor. I have no idea who, what, when. But I can tell you this, I used to go back to see the same person all the time. I think she owned it, quite frankly. Hand job, I think would be the best description. Well, you know, it was a little naughty. I don't know how else to put it. I knew I'd done something a little different. I think my wife did figure it out, but we never discussed it.

Well it's kind of strange the way I got there. I went in for just plain pleasure, and the suggestion was made over and over, "Do this, try that." And so I did. I think it was the eighties. I was looking for pleasure, but into the unusual. I found them interesting. And I think in retrospect it was because *they* were bored. It was as much for their benefit, if you will, or for their distraction as for mine.

Mechanical? Oh God, the odds were pretty good that that's how it would end up. And in retrospect, I can understand. What might be exciting for you or I is just humdrum for them. Oh yes, I saw women experience pleasure too.

No, the only thing I worried about, and it depended where I was, was my physical safety. Some of these places are absolutely new to me, so I'm walking down alleys I don't know about.

It was easy to have an erection because I was already halfway there before I would go. It's already there if you will. Only once did I lose an erection. I told about it to someone and they said, "Oh, she's a cocaine head." Cause she was acting paranoid. So I got the answer. She was acting really weird, saying "They're knocking at the door." I was just observing. Yes, we were in her home. The use of drugs is unbelievable, and that's when everybody was party-hardy. They were everywhere. Everywhere. And once someone knew you, they were very casual about the whole thing. I never took any drugs, but I'm talking about what was going on around me. When I realized that someone wasn't all there, it made me nervous. Anybody who hears things that aren't there, that should be a clue. I tried to leave, but she was so crazy that she thought they were spying on her, so she wouldn't let me near the door. So I thought, I'll humor this person because I want to get out of here alive. I know it sounds humorous, but there was something so off-color about what was going on. I don't trust those people. It's not that I'm afraid of them. I don't trust them.

I've had hundreds of experiences, probably. I see someone now maybe once a week. The only thing that would slow me down now is a question of cost. I've been divorced for years. I like my private parts played with obviously. Jesus, I'm going to get slapped for this (mutters). Um, you know, I like, penetrating them. I like oral, hand, vaginal, anal. Do I like to be penetrated? Maybe I would under certain circumstances. It's not what I'm running for or to. Yes, I only see fetish sex workers. You see, what used to be a real profession is now just a hooker who can't work anywhere else. So if you see them, they're terrible, because they're hustlers. They pretend to be fetish workers, and they're not. Or they used to call them Kittens with whips, or something like that. No, I'm not a submissive. I enjoy the shuffle. That's it. Well, I'll tell you, I like external play, but at the end of the day I enjoy, if I can, pleasuring them.

There's a certain component of power, I guess, and if you talk to someone who's never done it before, they get angry at almost any suggestion you make. And that's a buzz-killer, trust me. It's kinky. It's not like a farm girl laying down in the hay. I like things a little unusual here or there. You see, I'm very much a control person in my regular life, I mean very much in control, and if somebody really and truly tries to control me, I laugh. I mean I actually start laughing, because it is something that will never happen. And so if it's being done, it has to be done on a more subtle basis. I realize I'm being told what to do without someone screaming at me.

No, I'm not currently having sex with non sex workers but I get something extra out of playing- it's the naughty factor. That's just the best way to describe it.

You see, when I started playing, the people who played professionally, were players, in other words, they enjoyed doing it and I enjoyed getting it, and a little back and forth. What's going on now is, some of them are just hookers, because they can't do anything else, and the scene, as they say, has changed. For a while it was a fad, and people were doing it because it was a fad. But now it's, I wouldn't say it's run by pimps, I wouldn't be surprised, because that's kind of the attitude. It's quite distant.

The other thing you should know is, if you're doing research on who these people are, you have to keep in mind that a lot of them are Asian, who are involuntary servitude. I mean, they came over here, someone got them in it, and now they're paying for it. And I mean that. That's not an exaggeration. Yes, in the massage parlors. But that's a different group of people. And I don't know if you could draw the same conclusions because most of those people, unfortunately, are not here voluntarily. And it upsets me because there's nothing I can do about it. I just wanted to make that clear to you so you don't run afoul of the things that be. I've been around long enough to know it's there, and it's always going to be there. But one of the things that's interesting is, a lot of the players, women, don't want it recognized, because that kills the mystique. And so even though they talk about it, when you really talk to them about it, they prefer things just the way they are. They want sex work to be naughty or a bit promiscuous, a little bit away from what you should be doing, but not dealing with murder. The ones I know, don't really care about the law. They're smart enough to know, if the neighbors complain, you move on. But none of them are out there crusading. None that I know of. Just as long as there's no trouble, everything's fine. And that's what I really see. You know everybody says, we're being oppressed, but most of them have been playing so long, they know that's not really the case. Every six months or so, the police raid the place, and it's strictly for publicity. And I know that for a fact because they arrest somebody, and they tell whoever they're going to arrest early, because they don't want any trouble. And they say to him, bring along your phone or whatever, and they book them under a phony name. Because the cops are perfectly happy to see them going on. It's just one less person that they have to deal with in reality. They'd just as rather have people see sex workers. It cuts down on their problems. Well they don't have to do anything. They don't have guys out there molesting women and this and that. It makes the whole town, it makes everybody get some relief. And many, many of the clients are the police. I just know for a number of reasons, including having to straighten one out, who had some wrong ideas about what he was up to.

There are people who just don't like things. And the more they think you are enjoying yourself, the less they like it. And you can see that in so many different areas, including kids that want to

go skateboarding. They don't like people who enjoy themselves.
So what if it's suppressive to women? That doesn't mean you can
control it? It doesn't mean you can solve it. The truth is, if there
were simple solutions, they would have taken already. There are a
lot of people that walk around, that are like balloons of anger.
And the one that pops that balloon, gets all the anger. I would say,
1) it's none of your business. 2) it's a perfectly natural urge.
People like what they like.

And there's another element here. There are a lot of wives
who are just as happy as can be that their husbands are going to a
sex worker. It's one less thing that they have to worry about. They
may not like it anymore, they may never have liked it.

Joshua

Eugene, 2005

I should give you some background which is kind of
interesting. I was kind of late coming into sexuality to begin with.
I was still a virgin at the age of 23. And then it was hard finding
girlfriends, things like that. And then at 23, I became a born again
Christian, and in doing so I decided on a life of monogamy, but I
needed to be married first sort of thing, and all of that in my brain.
And so for ten more years I remained a virgin because I couldn't
find a partner to get married to and all of that. Subsequently, so I
didn't even have sex until I was 33. And that was after I
abandoned Christianity and other religions and became an atheist.
And that was about the year 2000.

So it's funny I was born in 1966 and I didn't even have sex
until the twenty-first century. It's really frustrating, but yeah. And
my first sexual encounters were with girls I dated here and there. I
was only with two women before I finally did get married, and
the woman I married was a virgin. So then I was married, and we
both were very inexperienced. She had been a Mormon and I had
been a born again Christian, but we both kind of adopted more
secular views after we got married. And because we were both so
inexperienced I think we just thought there was something more
out there. So we became swingers eventually. And in that lifestyle
I was totally nothing. She would get sex all the time and I was
just, I didn't have any resentment, I was happy for my wife, I
wanted her to be pleased and pleasured and things like that, but I
didn't know what I was doing. And my wife endorsed me going to
see sex workers. My wife actually made more money than me and
a few different times she actually even paid for it because I guess

she felt sorry for me if anything. I wasn't like trying to guilt trip her, I mean I'd maybe sit in the corner and cuddle with a girl, if I even had a girl next to me. I just didn't even know how to do sex. My wife and I were married seven years and we maybe had sex twenty-five times. I mean it was crazy.

So I had gone to strip clubs and things like that before, but I'd never partaken in anything except visual or a little bump-and-grind sort of thing, but there was a club here in my city that actually kind of doubled as a brothel even though it wasn't advertised that way, and my wife was aware of me going there. So when I went, I was able to have some sexual relations with some of the dancers there and it was really uplifting and gave me confidence, if you will, to get along better in the swinger community, or be more successful if you will. But then, I did meet one woman who just changed my life. I'll call her S, her initial was S, and she was an escort and I found her online, but I did my research, I didn't want to just, "Oh, she's a hot girl, I want to have sex with her." I wanted to find someone who could coach me or kind of teach me things that I didn't know. So I went on some different boards and things and I found this one girl that did that sort of thing. Sorry if I use that term girl, I'm old. She wasn't a girl, she was a woman.

Anyway, so when I met her, my first encounter with her was mostly just talking and we had a really good conversation. But when we did engage in sexual activity it just gave me all this confidence, and it planted a kink seed in me. I know that sounds silly, but I didn't realize that I had fetishes and things like that. And she brought those out in me. We explored them and she told me that there were local "munches." So in the kink community they have meet and greets for different people who are kinky and they are social gatherings and they call them munches. They're non-sexual, but they are ways to socialize with other people in that community. So she told me about this, and I was like "Wow, this sounds really interesting." So I became a little more interested in kink, but I didn't know what I was doing, and you don't want to jump into that. You need to learn before you start roleplaying or using impact or things like that with someone. So sex work basically opened me up to being more successful in my sexual identity because I started understanding kink and I eventually became a "Daddy." S is in the kink community and I stayed friends with her, though I never went back to her as a prostitute after we became friends, because I think it was too awkward. Plus I don't think she was doing that anymore. As friends we'd hang out and watch the stars and stuff without doing anything sexual, like it became completely platonic. It was kind of nice, you know?

So now I'm a little more experienced and my wife and I were having a hard time as swingers, you know, where we have to meet a couple where I like the girl and she likes the guy, so we decided to open up our marriage a little more and seek partners individually, or we didn't need to find couples in other words. So I started communicating with this girl south of where I live, about forty miles away who told me she had a "Daddy," and I was like, "What is that?" I thought it was kind of creepy initially, you know the whole calling somebody "Daddy," I just didn't get it. And she explained to me that it's a dynamic that they have, and it's a power exchange, but that's for a different story- kink. But in doing so she told me she was going to be coming to a hotel party that a local swinger's club was putting on. So I met her there and my wife went off, and I'm still nervous not knowing what I'm doing, and I kind of looked at her and said jokingly, cause we'd been talking a lot back and forth online on Adult Friend Finder and chat, back in the day when we did chat on our computers, "Hey, if nobody's going to get this party started, I am!" and I just kind of grabbed her and threw her over my shoulder. I mean it wasn't like I scared her, she was giggling the whole time, we were just frolicking and I was being jokingly aggressive with her, you know what I mean? And she's giggling and she totally ate it up and I had no idea that some women like to have aggression used toward them because I had always been taught, "You don't do that," you know? She had hinted to me enough that she was into that, so it wasn't like I was scaring her or whatever. So I learned from her too, though she wasn't a sex worker, but she was in the kink community, so she brought this all to me.

So we were messing around and I threw her down on the bed. I wasn't slapping her face or anything or being overly aggressive (at that point I had never even explored something like that with a woman). Then after we had sex, she went and had sex with other men, but then she would always crawl back on my lap and kind of sit with me, and that's when the "Daddy" part of me really came out. And so I understood, it was like a big revelation, almost a religious experience for me where I'm like, "Oh, my gosh this is something I kind of like. This is something I fetishize." So that was my spark to explore kink and then I went to these munches that the S girl had told me about, and then I became way more successful in sexuality at kinky things because I learned to be a "Daddy-Dom." So in doing all that I joined sex positive groups and I understood how my repressed sexuality due to my religion and stuff was something I wanted to fight against. It's not like, oh everyone should have sex, but everyone should have the freedom to do what they want sexually.

So it didn't destroy our marriage but it made it so that we weren't sexually compatible because, well the S girl that taught me these things, I'm sure her motives were to help me enhance my marriage with my wife, but it didn't work that way because I discovered kink and my wife was not kinky. So we ended up doing different things. She would go to swingers' parties and I would go to kink parties. And they often were at the same place, but we wouldn't engage with each other so it made our marriage non-sexual with each other. I mean we were both having crazy amounts of sex, it just wasn't with each other. I was completely happy with it, but given the power dynamic, which is an odd thing, it didn't work out.

I can't even remember the physical things I did with the first sex worker I saw because it was all so cerebral. I know we had sex and it was $300 for sixty minutes. With the sex workers from the strip club, it was always just penetrative sex, but it was interesting because I've never been able to have sex where I'm sitting and the girl sits down on me except with these stripper girls. Like all other partners I've ever had I've always taken the initiative and done doggie-style or missionary, hard fucking that way or whatever. But with these girls you're in a different position, you're prone, laid back and your penis is up and they were able to sit on me and do that which I've never been able to do. I mean I've tried with other partners and it has never even worked, so it's kind of funny, like their skills, if you will, make it possible. They made me more comfortable. I have more confidence with them I think. I don't think I ejaculated with any of them though. I don't know if it's due to my diabetes or due to my repressed sexual, messed up stuff in my head, but I've always had problems ejaculating with anything but masturbation until I met a recent partner. And condoms are really not easy for me. I maybe have ejaculated into a condom, like five times in my entire life. So I have to have a fluid-bonded partner in order to ejaculate with vaginal intercourse and I've had maybe five in my whole life. But I've had sex over hundred different times with a hundred different women. So usually ejaculation doesn't ever happen for me. And I always use a condom, because that's just what you do. Except for oral, I will admit, I've had sex workers do oral with me without a condom.

So when I've had lulls in my life, like not been dating or not had a partner, I have gone back to sex workers for kind of a retro boost to get back in my game, if you will. Because I really, I mean this is bad, it's probably mental issue, but I sometimes feel like nobody wants me. And it's like, if I'm able to have sexual relations with someone, even if I'm paying them, that doesn't matter in my head, I can separate it and I can still feel wanted and needed and that sort of thing. There wasn't any discomfort after the good experience people I've been with, but I have been with some people that were bad experiences, which I'm sure you want me to discuss, too. This one was interesting, it was before I was married, and I never had actual sex with any of these people, but I actually went to Nashville, and I was still hadn't had sex yet, and I was still a Christian, but new to being a hedonist, if you will, and the strippers there were a lot different than the strippers where I live. I went to Nashville with my mom of all people, but I went off on my own and one of the things I did was went to the strip clubs there. And the first thing I did when I walked in was ask the bouncer what the rules were, because I knew they were different in different parts of the country, and he says, "Um, you just can't touch their pussies." I was like, "Whoa, okay." So sure enough, I get there, and first of all it's weird there, you bring your own booze, and they sell you a glass of ice, and then basically you get two songs, not one song, and you get to put your hands all over these girls, even your mouth on their breasts, whatever you want to do for the entire time. And you get two songs for $15! Like I'm not kidding. Versus where I live it was $20 for one song and they couldn't even touch you legally at all. So it was such a big difference.

So after I had this extremely exciting sexual experience, it was super fun and I came back to my city hoping to find the same thing, and the closest I could come up with were these things called lingerie modeling shops, which I know that prostitution does happen in these sometimes, but they also are, but it's not suppose to happen, it's suppose to be the man masturbates while the girl dances in front of him, that's the legal thing that's suppose to happen there. But I was hoping for at least a little bit of touching, and I was used to paying $7.50 for three minutes. So I get in there and they want $40, which I thought was fair, so I put down $40 and I'm expecting this girl to do that, and she says, "No, that goes to the house. If you want anything more, you need to tip me." And I understand, but it wasn't made very clear, which is another reason I want prostitution legalized because it's so bad for people because consent and negotiation is part of consent and if you have to lie because the law makes you lie, than how are you ever going to have consent? You're never going to have consent. And every act of illegal prostitution is rape. Do you know what I mean? It makes it really fucked up. If prostitution was legal than every transaction could be documented specific to what the people want and there would be consent. That's one of the reasons I want prostitution legalized, it's so sad.

So that girl, I was hoping she would let me touch her, and she said, well you have to tip me, so I just threw down a five dollar bill thinking, "Okay, here's a tip," and she just rolled her eyes, turned around and turned the tape off and says, "We're through." But it was like, I get it, but I didn't get it because nobody told me. I get that you need to tip at least $40 if the girls are going to put their bodies against you, and then if you're going to want a hand job or a blow job or sex, if the girl even does that, which I've found after spending money, not even every girl does that, but if you do want that you have to put up at least a lot more money. So it was weird the culture shock. I wonder, in the South, because of they are religious, being the Bible belt and all, if it's a part of their culture to take more advantage of women that way. You know, they make them do dances fully nude against your body for only $7.50 a song and women are just used to it because that's how it is in the South. I don't know. It got me thinking. We have a lot of strip clubs in my city, so I've been able to go to different ones to find out how they work and only a few of them have doubled as brothels. I was worried about the illegality when I was really young, and kind of when I was married, because it would jeopardize my ex-wife's career, I didn't really have a career. It didn't dissuade me. It just made it more difficult. Because I would like to just call somebody up and negotiate it and do it. But you can't even talk about it because you're not supposed to really be doing it. It's just so frustrating.

I felt really angry initially after that, but I've grown to understand that the issue wasn't her being a bad person or me. It was a misunderstanding. She had *no* way of telling me without it jeopardizing her. If I was a cop, I mean she can't tell me, "If you pay me $60 I'll rub your cock." She can't say that, and I can't know that either. There are all these unspoken things. And that's what I hate about it so much is that. And it's not because the girls don't want it and it's not because the guys don't want it, it's because the law is the way it is and it's really messed up. So that girl, after she said, "We're done," she kept the money obviously, so I did feel kind of robbed then, and she said if I complained she would call the police so I just let it be. I've had a lot of girls I've talked to and we were supposed to meet up and we never met up.

Well I've gone and met people initially online who I thought might be kind of fun and when I met them I either wasn't attracted to them or we didn't mesh too well. I've always paid them anyway because you don't want to get a bad reputation, and it's not their fault I'm not attracted to them, right? I mean nobody has really tried to mislead me. And then a couple of times more recently, the last time I went to see somebody, about a year ago, I didn't have sex with her, I wanted to, but I just couldn't bring myself to do it. I didn't get a good enough erection, and I don't know, I still had my ex-girlfriend on my mind, I think. She was an ex, I mean, she should have been a total ex because she was really cruel in the way she broke up with me. She posted pictures of her new boyfriend with a condom wrapper on the floor and his hands all around her online on the date that we broke up. It was really cruel. So it lowered my self-esteem a lot after that experience, so that's why I went back to the sex workers to try to get it back. But my girlfriend was so beautiful that it was hard to find a sex worker that was as beautiful as my girlfriend was, and she wasn't, so I couldn't go through with it. I did get oral sex from her. She was really aggressive when I met her at her house, she like kissed me before I even paid her or was in the door, which I liked. She came up and gave me a huge hug and kissed me out of the blue and told me to go change and wash up in the bathroom if I needed to, I wasn't dirty or anything obviously. So I knew I wanted to engage with her, but when it got time to "get down to business" if you will, she was not attractive to me. She was very hippy like, which isn't really the kind of person I like. She smelled like patchouli and had kind of dreaded hair, that kind of thing. Which isn't something that appeals to me. It's just kind of a "turn off," she wasn't an unattractive person or anything. So I couldn't have sex with her but she gave me oral sex and finished me with her hand and I actually came. I've gone to other sex workers just for hand jobs and stuff. But it's way too expensive it's like $150 bucks for that, it's crazy.

In my life, total sex workers, maybe between 5-8 with

around 12 visits, unless you count strippers giving lap dances than it's probably in the hundreds, but as far as stuff where my cock gets touched or where I'm fingering her or fucking her that's what I would consider that. I mean watching a porn video is seeing a sex worker so it's hard to define it. It's not super common thing for me, I mean number one I work a minimum wage job and less than 40 hours a week, so financially is one big reason for that. Oh, and another thing too, is not just "are you afraid of the cops, it's are you afraid that the girl is going to rip you off, or not provide you what you're looking for?" I mean I would go to see a sex worker, not only just for sex, if I could negotiate that up front. If I could say, "Oh, let's not do fucking, but may I touch your nipples and caress you. This is what I'd like to pay you." I mean it'd be really nice to be able to do things like that too. But because the laws are so vague you can't negotiate a damn thing and you just have to put the money down and see what happens. And if you push too far you're in danger of "raping" somebody and that's really scary. I mean I'm really concerned. I don't want to do something without consent.

So after I became kinky and after I got my divorce, I had a girlfriend who actually worked as a prostitute, and she actually lived with me. It was interesting, she was my partner in sex and kink but then she would see other men for money. But because my ex-wife still owned half of the house, that was one of the reasons we broke up because no one was comfortable with her doing that in the house. Because if she had gotten in trouble, it would have reflected poorly on my ex-wife if she still owned the house. So we ended up having to split up and we just became friends. But she wanted to have an in-call location and I was fine with her doing it here, I mean, I've always loved sex workers, and I didn't mind it, I mean it was kind of hot to have a girlfriend that was a sex worker to be honest. This was the same as the S girl, she was very much in it because she was an overly sexual person and she liked to help people. I mean we used to go to sex clubs together and find guys that we could tell were kind of sad or had never had sex. I guess you could say I was like her pimp, but we weren't making money for this because we were doing it for like, compassion for other people. Because my life, like growing up and not having sex until I was 35 and all that, I felt sorry for them, and here I have a girl who is real open sexually so I would take her and share her with a lot of people. It was really fun and I felt really good for that. But some people we would meet were like being given away in arranged marriages and stuff so they had no clue what they were going to do. I mean if you're just some Indian guy who's never really had sex and is getting ready to get married, I mean I felt really for them. So I would share her with him, and she liked that sort of thing. She wanted to help people with her sexuality. And to be paid for it was good, but it wasn't her motive. So that was one of the reasons I liked her so much. I still love her. She's still a good friend.

I also see women unhappy in their job all the time actually, and if I do, I don't pursue those sorts of women, because if I do, I'd be adding to their pain. It's really tough to explain how I know. It's the way they engage towards me. I mean, I could be wrong, there could be a woman who's really in pain and is just really good at being a sex worker or whatnot, but I usually try to talk to them about it. It's all back to that consent thing. If she shows an interest in me and what I'm talking about, then I'm like, "okay, are you interested in more, sort of thing?" It's hard to explain, that wasn't a very good answer. A lot of them, you can just tell, and I don't want to stereotype just so that you know what my thought process is, but if they kind of feel like they're a "tweeker" (I don't want to use that term), but if you can tell they're real haggard or something, you can tell they're probably in pain and they're doing it out of a necessity rather than out of a love for doing it. I mean drugs are used by everybody I know, except me, I don't use drugs or drink. It's funny, but if things are getting to the point where I can tell they're doing it for a necessity to live rather than a necessity to live. And I can ask that question: "Are you dancing because you enjoy being a dancer and dancing and being sexual or are you dancing because you need the money?" Most girls can answer that and I can usually ask that without it sounding like I'm a cop or something. I mean they don't say, "Oh well you don't have to pay." And I feel like I should compensate them because they're providing me with a service I can't provide myself and they're providing me with a service that I value above almost anything in the whole world. I mean that's probably misguided, I should probably value other things more, to be honest, sexual pleasure as a hedonist is something I value more than anything.

No, I don't see myself seeing sex workers for the rest of my life. I mean it will always be on the table if needed, but I don't have any plans to see one right now at all or for the rest of my life, but at the same time, if I get to a place where I want that, or if it becomes legal or if I go to a place where I'm comfortable, I'll do it again, no problem. In all honesty, I'm not having any sex right now. But I have a girl on the horizon that I might be dating here, so I'm feeling happy engaging in that. Sometimes when you're just real lonely you don't have any, I mean I think a lot of the times I went to see sex workers I would have been just as happy, if not happier to go on a first date with a potential lover. Because being with prostitutes is a dead end. I mean I don't usually think I'm going to see a sex worker to have a relationship. So you want the sex, the sex is nicer, it's nice to have that. It kind of brings it all together. Then again, I've still not had my most ultimate sexual experience that's still in my head that I always want. Well it's not even an experience, it's a perfected sex. You know how most men will fuck for a while and then just come really well. There are certain women that I find so attractive that I can get an erection without ever being touched. But I've never been with a woman like that ever. I've seen them in movies, and I've seen them in strip clubs, but as far as engaging with them, it's been something I've always wanted. So I'm kind of looking for this elite prostitute that I find so attractive that I can just have this amazing orgasmic experience while fucking. And I've never found that and it's not easy, because if you're that gorgeous you're going to fetch $1000 a session and I can just never afford that. Maybe I could find it dating, maybe, but I mean it's not easy to find women to date that I find somewhat attractive. As a daddy, too, and coming into sexuality so late in life, I'm kind of messed up because I don't really find women my age attractive, which is really sad. Like I'm

51 and I hardly even find women in their forties attractive. Usually they have to be under 35. And like the last girlfriend that broke up with me, she was 22. So you know, that whole "daddy" thing is a big deal for me.

So one thing that I would say is super important is the whole consent issue. Because of the way the laws are, it makes it impossible for true, honest, enthusiastic consent to be ever be done. Which maybe means I shouldn't even do it at all, but that doesn't mean that I should, because it should be legal. It's a good thing to share sexuality with other people. Whether for money or not, it doesn't matter, it's a good thing. And there are all sorts of good things we spend money on, so why would that not be one. Sexuality feels good. It's uplifting. It brings my mood up, and it's a natural antidepressant. It's an esteem booster, too. But if you do it wrong, it could be all the opposite of those things, and maybe for the women it's a depressant, it's a demoralizer, that's why it needs to be entered into with enthusiastic consent.

Derek

Los Angeles, 1998

I should have listened to my inner voice that said, "No. Don't do it." I had a patient once who had connections to the underworld, and on top of that, was a hustler and a very good salesman. He persuaded me to hire his "friend" to come over to my place and "cheer me up," after I had broken up with my girlfriend.

The lady was pretty, all right, but her breath stunk like cigarettes. She wanted the money laid on the table – up front – and announced that her driver was waiting downstairs for her to finish, and that she was ready to suck me off. Jesus! What a turn-off.

So there she was, working her mouth on my dick for about an hour, while every thought but my own pleasure went through my mind. I don't remember getting hard even once. I worried that she might think me gay or not normal or not much of a man. Did she enjoy having a dick in her mouth? Tick, tick, tick. . .my, how time drags when you're not having fun! Without some kind of personal connection, "sex" for me is a complete waste of time (and money, in this case.)

Finally the hour was up. I apologized and put my penis back in my underwear. She scoffed, took the money, and left. And so, for the first — and definitely the last — time in my life, I had paid for sex.

Kamil

Paris, 2000

So I don't remember why but my friend said that I had to sleep with a prostitute, which I refused to do. And I don't know why that night I was like, "Okay, fine. I'll do it." So I went to the sixteenth arrondissement and I picked the least attractive one of all. Like this really overweight African woman, but she looked reassuring, healthy and motherly, knowing that I would not be attracted to her whatsoever. I don't know if we were in my car or if she picked me up, and she drove me to a street where she thought that we wouldn't be seen by anyone, and she told me to put my car seat down, so I did, and then I realized that the street I was on you could see the Eiffel Tower between my legs. So I'm sitting back and the Eiffel Tower is between my legs, and this really nice, fat African woman put a condom on my limp dick and tried to suck it for like five minutes before I told her, "You can keep the money, I want this over and done with." And that was that. That was my only ever experience with a prostitute, and my first and my last.

Jared

New York, 2003

I don't remember chronologically, it's all kind of a haze. More recent is probably more fresh than the former, but I'd say the first time was probably in my early twenties. It felt exciting. I sought it out myself on the Internet. I think the first few times was probably a rub-and-tug type situation, where you go to a massage parlor and you choose a woman, you pay her, and you go in the back with her and pay her additionally for anything extra. The first few times I went there, business was highly "upsell-ish." A hand job was definitely available but there was an enticement for more, but it wasn't very realistic. It was usually easy to have an erection and an orgasm, but I can remember a couple of times, yeah, just generally with a sex worker, I don't know about that environment specifically. Sometimes there's disinterest on both parts and its really mechanical, other times it felt like a pressured situation for time. I'd say generally it would be one of those two things. When I first started, sex felt potentially accessible with women, but not a certainty. And it was simpler with a sex worker. I didn't feel terribly preferential around physical characteristics. I think one of the things that was exciting was being with a woman who may have been more dominant. That was interesting to me at that time.

Generally it's been more going to see escorts now in my thirties. They will get a hotel room, and it costs more, and you're paying by the hour, but more is available than a hand job, though it varies from woman to woman. I've also purchased sex abroad in Amsterdam and in Prague. Those have been sort of different circumstances than seeing escorts in hotels here. One of the difficult things is you're calling someone up from the Internet to purchase basically an illegal service, so it's very difficult to ascertain any details on either side. Have you ever put up an ad to

sell a piece of furniture on Craigslist? Where both sides are trying
to figure out if the other side is real because there's this
incredulity about it because it's happening over Craigslist. So this
is sort of similar with things getting "sussed" out over the phone
and they don't want to convey any specifics about services they
provide because they're concerned it could be the police on the
other side of the line. Similarly from the client's side, I may have
a specific request, or something like that, but I have to go see
them in person and figure it out rather than being about to
negotiate x, y or z service with a consenting adult in exchange for
money.

I typically pay $200- $400 an hour. There are also some
ladies offering services by the half hour. I use condoms every
time. I'm pretty vigilante about that, especially in that type of a
situation. I notice that female pleasure varies quite a bit. It's
something that I have a bit of attention on. It really affects the
experience, how the women relate to it. So like, for example,
there are times where there is obvious disinterest, sort of accepted
moaning or things that are highly unrealistic, and then there are
ones that feel really turned on, like her body is giving physical
signs like, her face is getting red and her vagina is wet, those kind
of things. So yeah, it really varies. In a lot of cases, the money is
part of it, and you pay up front, but once you're having sex, it's
just two people having sex. I imagine they turn down clients here
and there but I imagine they are more or less agreeable to having
sex with anyone, but sometimes feel very averse, or disgusted
perhaps, and other times feel into it.

Not during, but at the outset, there have been some times
when like when I've gone to someone's place the situation has
seemed unsafe or unsavory, like before even starting I've left.
There are also plenty of times I've left and felt shame or remorse
about it. It comes from a complex variety of things. I'm sure some
of it is it's a place to manifest personal shame, others are society's
notion that it's wrong, others are, it's so many things. Yes, my
partner thinks, we have a funny dynamic around it. For myself,
it's this thing that usually there is some excitement and it's sort of

this compulsive tendency for me, not like a smoking habit that I do everyday, at this point it's just a couple of times a year at most, maybe once a year, but it feels like this compulsive thing that will usually happen when I've been drinking, like it's sort of unconscious. Not just the shame, but for several reasons I've decided it's just not generally something I want to be doing anymore. I will do it and I'll have a good time while I'm doing it, but I'll have mixed feelings about it afterwards. And then, my girlfriend she sort of recognizes it as such. Her thing is she wants me to not feel shame about it. It's not upsetting to her that I do it, so long as I'm honest about it. If I'm not than it's, like if I keep it a secret than it's very upsetting to her. But if I'm honest she's really nonchalant about it. And then there's other times where we've been out and she thought it might be something fun to do together, and that's where I recognize that it's a compulsion in that it's this secret thing that I do alone. It's a secret, compulsive type of thing. There's some piece in there about confidence. I don't see anything overtly wrong on either side with a man paying a woman for sexual services, but there is also this piece of it which relates to how women relate to me, and it could be some reminder of bad self-worth psychology. Meaning I feel like my only worth or attraction to women is through money.

Yes, I'm in an open relationship, so both me and my partner can have other partners. And to be clear most of my other partners are female friends or not full-on girlfriends, but more like mistresses, that type of thing. At this point my activities with sex workers are pretty limited. I think essentially what I wanted to do was to be able to have that novelty and excitement that is really strong in that experience, but to have something similar. There's also the piece where there's a lot of freedom in it. It sounds kind of shitty, I guess, but you're having an experience with someone who you don't really know, you may, depending on how it goes, there's no compulsion to see each other again. So it certainly feels very freeing and there are little specific things that you may like that you may feel are too vulnerable to convey to a lover the first few times you're going to sleep with them and you're concerned about turning them off. That was one of the things that I really connected with sex workers, because they're not uncomfortable talking about that. I mean, they may judge you, people are people, that doesn't go away, but it's different where you have this anonymous experience with a stranger and they don't know who you are and you don't have to feel the weight of their judgment. I really like for a woman to sit on my face and play with my cock at the same time, and depending on what my perceptions of the new lover are, it may feel really taboo to ask for. And I usually like for a woman to pull on my nipples extremely hard. So I'll usually request those types of things, and I know it's fairly standard, like it's not off the deep end, compared to some of the requests they get. And I know those things are more and more a part of normal sex acts all the time so I'd say for me it's getting less vulnerable or uncomfortable for me to make those things in a sex experience I'm not paying for.

Sebastian

Reno, 1985

I would have been about 25 years old. Well, wait a
second, with a sex worker, okay, I got to go way back then. I was
born and raised in Reno, which as you know, Mustang Ranch is
15 miles outside of Reno. So when I turned 16 years old I was
shanghaied by my friends at about midnight and taken to Mustang
Ranch on my birthday. And that was my first experience, and it
scared the hell out of me, because I had no idea what I was doing,
and I was still a virgin, and I was still a virgin afterwards. I was
really, really nervous and I felt really weird about the whole
thing, to this day, which is funny. I think I asked for a hand job.
Back in the day you had like a half an hour limit, and I really
ended up talking to her most of the time, and by the time we got
around to it, I was still so nervous that nothing could happen. I
was scared to death. First of all I was 16 years old and the county
sheriff was sitting at the bar. Little did I know that it was legal in
Nevada at age 16, you just couldn't have a drink. But they never
told us that so we just saw there were multiple sheriffs sitting at
the bar and thought, oh my god we're going to get arrested. So we
were all kind of freaked out. And the madam rushed us into the
rooms saying, "You guys can't be out here, you need to get into a
room." So I was already nervous, it was late at night, and more
than anything else, I am a hopeless romantic and I've always
wanted those kind of experiences to be with someone I cared
about. I think the woman was nervous also because I was so
young. She was young too, probably in her early twenties, and
she was very kind, but they run that place like "clock work," so
when your time was up the door was getting knocked on and you
were done. That was the only part to me was that she was

constantly pressuring me to stop talking and move on. And what she didn't realize is that I really didn't want to do anything. I was perfectly comfortable not doing anything which is basically what happened.

And more importantly, what you should know about me, is I was raised a very sexually repressed Catholic. Which is why I'm so messed up. Yes, masturbation was not allowed, and that was one of the biggest problems. It was a sin, you were sick, and by that point in time I was already very sadistic and I already had fetishes. I'm a leather fetishist, because most of the images that I have identified with that I found early on, that I identified to be dominant women, were of women wearing leather. So I developed that fetish. About a year prior to that, I was 15 and I had this little bag of leather things in my car. Actually I was 16, that my mother found and it was like the world was going to come to an end, I was sick, and I needed to go see a psychologist. And I had already, when I was about 12 or 13 I was playing with myself in the bathroom, I didn't even know what masturbation was, and my brother picked the lock and came in there and I was laying on the floor naked playing with myself and of course that went through the family like wild fire and even then they told me what was wrong with me, and that I was clearly sick. Not a healthy upbringing when it comes to sexuality.

My fetish fantasies started when I was probably about eight to ten years old. I went to Catholic school my entire life and when I was in fifth grade, so I would have been eleven, the principle of the school was taking me into her office as punishment. And something more obviously, every day I was suppose to come to her office, she would draw the blinds and close the windows, and she would make me strip naked and she would paddle me in her office as punishment for forgetting my lunch money or for being late paying my lunch money. But I always thought that was kind of the point in my life in which I became submissive because I actually liked that. I liked the attention and I liked being submissive to her and the sexual touching that was happening while it was going on. But I always felt guilty about it a bit. I carried a lot of guilt up until about a year ago. Anyway so that was kind of a life event for me, but what I've identified recently is that I was already submissive prior to that. And I suspect that my submissiveness is what made her feel comfortable enough that she would do that to me and instruct me not to tell my parents and that I wouldn't. Because it went on for several months before it slipped out one day that this was occurring and my parents immediately got upset and pulled me out of the school and moved me to a different Catholic school.

But I really think my submissiveness goes way, way back to early, I want to say four, five or six years old. I recently identified, when in some deep introspection, that I remembered that when I was in Kindergarten or a little older, the girl down the street from me who lived on the corner, we used to play together, and it got to the point where, she had one of those big play sets in her backyard with a hidden, covered under part, and we would go under there every day and she would play nurse and patient with me. And make me pull my pants down and sit on my hands and investigate me. Something kids do, but in my mind, the more I thought about it, in order for her to feel comfortable enough for that to happen I must have been giving off signals that I was submissive and of course for her to be somewhat dominant.

The next experience was when I was 22 and I went with a group of friends out to Mustang Ranch as a Bachelor party thing because I was about to get married. So they took me out there and said, we'll pay for it, you do whatever you want to do. And once again I was really uncomfortable and I didn't want to do a whole lot, even though at this time I was far less nervous about the situation, so I ended up getting a hand job. And the girl I remember very distinctly, she was absolutely beautiful, stunningly beautiful, very sweet, and it didn't take long before I was satisfied. Well again because of my submissiveness, the discomfort and the goofy hopeless romantic that's in me and the ridiculous Catholic upbringing, I wanted to experience that with someone that I care deeply about (and I'm still this way today). I don't have to have sex, I want to feel, not necessarily in love with the person but I want to care about them and know them. You can count on less than one hand my total number of one-night experiences in my life. I'm just weird that way. I'm goofy that way. I'm not the typical guy when it comes to wanting to just go out and have sex. I work in construction so it's a on the surface manly man industry and they all want to go to the strip clubs and have sex with sex workers, which is great, but that's just not my thing. I don't judge them for it. It's just not something I sit well with in that setting.

I enjoyed vaginal sex with partners but there always felt like there was something missing, until this day. So I got married really young as you can tell, and got married for the completely wrong reasons. Even though I had been mainly honest with her about my submissiveness and my desires and stuff like that and she had agreed to wear some leather for me, I was unsatisfied sexually. I was with a woman with whom I wanted to be submissive in the bedroom, and she didn't know how to do that. She didn't know how to be dominant. And in those days I thought it was more of a leather fetish thing than a dominant-submissive thing. So I believed it was more important that someone was willing to wear leather, while we were in that setting, naively, and I was wrong. So I was married to her for four years, and at the three-year mark, I went to a play party and it was the first time I had ever seen a public display of 'play'. And I actually saw women dominating men and I realized, although nothing happened with me, it rocked me to my core, that that is really what I want. I was traveling for work in Dallas, Texas of all places, and I was there for a week, and I found through one of the local newspapers an ad for a play party thing. So I went and it was, especially for someone like me, it was earth shaking. The problem was I didn't have any actual experiences. There was a girl there that was absolutely stunning, who I really wanted to experience something with, but I was very shy, and kept to myself, and I needed to work the next day, and about 1:30 in the morning I could barely keep my eyes open, and I got up to leave, and at that point, I'm guessing it was her boyfriend, husband, play partner – whatever, chased me to the door and said, "Hey, she wants to play with you." But it was too late and I said, "You know I'm really flattered, but I can't stay. I've got to go get some sleep and have to be at work at 6am." Shame on me I should have just made it an all-nighter. I didn't know it would be such a long time before I had another experience like that, hindsight being 20/20.

So that was the turning point for me when I started to put an image together of what I wanted. I wanted to be dominated in that setting, in a sexual setting. SO then my next experience was about three years later, about a year after my divorce. I had had plenty of dates and just not finding anybody with any interest in doing anything. So I decided to try a pro-domme. I was actually living in the LA area at the time. My first experience with a pro-domme was amazing. She was very young, and was at one of these places where the dungeon hosts the party and all the girls work there, they're not independent. It was an incredibly erotic experience for me, and I was very young at the time and I was extremely attracted to her, and I asked her out and she said yes. And I was really excited to take her to dinner, and like the day of or the day before she canceled. She got cold feet. I suspect she talked to a co-worker or something and they talked her out of it. And boy, that was earth-shattering when she backed out. I was so excited about it. And then after that I was kind of turned off by everything because I was heartbroken by that experience so it was several months again before I tried with a pro-domme. My next experience was not very good because she didn't listen to anything I had to say. I told her what my likes and dislikes were, and she crossed all my limits right away and it was just not a good experience. In fact, she was not in a very sanitary location, let's put it that way. It wasn't a very nice place, and I didn't get a sense of safety, and then what pushed me even further, she was older by the way, about not even five minutes into it, she wanted me to eat her pussy, go down on her, and I was not, just because of the setting, the newness, I wasn't comfortable, so I refused to do it. It was already one of my limits. I had told her that I didn't want to exchange bodily fluids or anything. Actually I think that was my third experience, because I remember I was so blown away that she wanted that because the others were so strict about no contact like that. So she really caught me off guard when she asked for that, and when I refused she got really upset and told me that I was suppose to do what she told me to do. It was just not a good experience and I ended up ending the session, paid her for the session, and just told her it wasn't what I wanted and went away.

So then it was another long break after that, because I was turned off from that experience. But I tried a couple of others, maybe six pro-dommes in about a five-year timeframe in which I was divorced. And then I met my current wife, and by this point in time I had matured enough to realized I wanted to be perfectly open with anybody that I dated, that I wanted to be upfront with what my needs and wants were, and if they didn't want me then let's move on. So when I met my wife, I was very open and came clean and she was like right on, sounds great, sounds like a lot of fun. She had been into riding Harleys, so she had already been into wearing leather, so she was like, "Leather, I love wearing leather." So things felt right from the very beginning with her. So we dated for a year and we got married. I was 33 by that time. Actually I was divorced for about seven years. So I was very clear with her that I had seen a dominatrix and everything. And we had a lot of fun. I mean she was growing into a role. And then, kids came, and she had always promised me she was going to be that person for me and after our kids were born, when my son was about three, so my daughter would have been about five, so about six years into the marriage, we've been married about fifteen years now, I was really, really, really depressed that once again I was feeling unfulfilled. And I was beginning to have thoughts of wanting to go see professional dommes again, so in almost an act of desperation, and I really worked hard to suppress all this stuff, so I was very suppressed at the time, so much so that I couldn't even talk to her about it anymore, and I had so many things to say, and I was so afraid of forgetting things that I ended up, on an airplane, on a job trip, I wrote a fifteen page letter basically trying to explain to her how critically important it was to me, and how depressed I was, for her to make the effort to want to fulfill my

needs that way, and midway on the flight home, when I was
changing planes at airports, I called her to check in and I was
balling. And she said,

"Oh my God, what's wrong?" And I explained to her that I
have to get something off my chest. And so I got home and I gave
her the letter and I ended up reading the letter to her as I was
balling the whole time, and so I finished the letter, and she was
like, "Oh, my God, is that all it is? Don't worry about that, it's
going to happen, we're going to go there. Everything is going to
be great." So I was reenergized and excited about the future
again.

Well, once again, nothing happened. I mean, nothing. The
most effort she made in our marriage was one time when she went
out and bought a book about becoming a dominatrix, or
something like that, but she never even really read any of it. So
things just really went on without change. And I didn't even
realize how deep of a depression that I went into, but I went into a
really, really deep depression. So about three years after nothing
happened, I finally decided I needed to have that in my life once
again so I started to see pro-dommes again. And I think I only
saw one before I met Mistress Jael. And the one before, it was an
okay experience, and I don't remember why I changed, but I
changed. So I met Mistress Jael and that first session with her was
just very different for me, very earth shattering. And I think this
will be shocking for you but, and it was even harder back then,
finding a pro-domme with a leather wardrobe was actually really
hard. Mistress Jael will tell you that the majority of her wardrobe
I supplied over the years. Because leather is expensive number
one, and number two, it's starting to come back into the scene, but
I think it got so associated with the male gay scene that it kind of
fell out of the scene for a while, everybody was into PVC or latex.
Now those things can do it for me too, but back then I was very
much a very strict leather fetishist. And that was really the
number one means in which I chose a professional domme. So
she had a decent wardrobe and I had a great experience. She is
one of a kind, literally.

So I started seeing her regularly. Now by that point I was living in Northern California and I was commuting back and forth regularly for work, which is when I would see her. I would see her in general once a month or once every other month. And then the next major life event happened. Even though I was seeing her, it was unrecognized even by myself, I was in a really, really deep depression. And what made me recognize how deep of a depression it was, two years ago, I got really sick in the summer time, they don't know if it was a stomach bug. I got pancreatitis associated with the gallbladder, and had to have my gallbladder removed and I was in the hospital for a month. And during that time, I had also let my body go. I was completely out of shape, never got any exercise, totally couch potato, didn't care about myself, didn't do anything, didn't eat right, didn't exercise, and I was very overweight. So then I go into the hospital extremely sick and lost about 40 pounds in that month while I was in and out of the hospital. But what I realized when I was in the hospital there were points when I was in there that I didn't care whether I lived or died. And that's when I identified I had a certain amount of apathy towards life. And I didn't know why. SO I get out of the hospital and even though I shed 40 pounds, I put 20 of them right back on in a fairly short period of time. And then about a year later I got back into my groove somewhat. And I was also very much a martyr- everybody else, taking care of wife and kids, was more important than me.

I started seeing Mistress Jael again and we had started getting closer and closer, like a friendship. And at one point, in September of last year, she had attended a class called MITT, short for masters in transformational training, and the best way to describe it is very, very deep introspection combined with a lot of Tony Robbins-ish self-empowerment type stuff, but really, really immersive. So she had gone through it, and she didn't know I was in this depression, but she had had such a great experience, that she suggested I try it. And I had never done any deep introspection like that. It's actually a weeklong basic class. And it's all about helping people identify how they got to where they are, why they are the way they are, their behaviors, and what they want to change about themselves, and how to do it. So then, I went through this and I came out of it absolutely mind blown, because during that week long period of time I realized how unhappy and depressed I was, and I realized it was more than anything else, because of the fact that I'm submissive and I've spent my entire life repressing it. I feel like I can almost sympathize with a gay person from the fifties. Because in modern US society, being a submissive male is not something we talk about. Though it's starting to become a little more mainstream, it drives me crazy because every submissive male in the movies, they are always stereotyped as weak, strange, weird guys. So I came out of that class realizing I'm almost suicidal because I'm submissive and I've spent my entire life burying this. I don't love myself and nobody loves the real me. Nobody even knows the real me, the only person who's even close to it is Mistress Jael.

So she and I started talking more and more about that and she really helped me to understand my feelings and help me realize how submissive I was and helped me realize what I wanted. So then two weeks later I decided to take the advanced course that starts giving you the tools to change. So I came out of that course a completely different person. On the day I came home I was 180 degrees from where I was going into it. I had chewed tobacco. Growing up in Reno in the eighties, I had chewed tobacco for 35 years and tried quitting multiple times, and I came home from that class a year ago and that day threw it away and never looked back. That very same day I told myself I love myself, I accept myself for who I am, and I'm a beautiful human being, and set a course that day to completely change my health, my body, and everything about how I live. Like I said I was a couch potato, so my de-stress mechanism was I would come home and after everybody went to bed I would watch TV or play video games from 10pm- midnight every night. That's how I would shut down. As of that day I immediately started working out five to six days a week, completely changed how I eat, cut all carbs out of my diet, and in a seven month period dropped sixty five pounds, and put on probably twenty-five pounds of muscle.

So if you were to see before and after pictures of me, people who see me today and knew me before, barely recognize me.

I've always been very, very highly sexed. Literally I could have sex every morning. But my drive went even crazier because I started feeling better about myself. So I wanted to be naked, and I was just proud of myself. And not only that, there was this massive weight that was lifted off my shoulders, because that same day that I changed everything about how I eat and live, I mean, my de-stress behavior now is I'm at the gym almost two hours everyday, but I came home and I talked to my wife. She won't admit it, but ever since we had the kids, she's become very sexually conservative. Because she's so worried about the kids seeing us or whatever, and she just became not sexual. She hasn't instigated sex in fifteen years. So I sat down and came clean. I told her I was unhappy, that I had been seeing professional dominatrixes for years, and I told her that if she couldn't find a way to be the person I thought she was going to be, who I believed I married, than we couldn't be together. Which was, you got to understand, the voice I found coming out of this whole thing, my power. So I was just very truthful, and told her, look, you don't love the whole me. You love part of me because you only know part of me. Of course it's been a very tough road. This all happened in October of last year. And there have been a lot of tears shed every time we have the conversation. I'm teary-eyed right now. But every time I have the conversation with her, it's a painful conversation, but it's a healthy conversation. She's an amazing person. We're trying to figure things out. We have our good days and our bad days. We're essentially living together vacillating together and apart. She knows about Mistress Jael and I've made a deal with her that at a bare minimum, if we are just staying together, that as my best friend in life, Mistress Jael, I'm closer with her than anyone I've been with in my entire life. She's truly my best friend, because she knows me and she loves me. She knows me inside out and she loves me for who I am, and I'm so grateful for that (crying). So the agreement I have with my wife is that no matter what happens Mistress Jael is my best friend and she's going to be in my life for the rest of my life. And it's still to be determined if she can. I told her, look, I have to let this out. I have to experience my submissive side, because if I repress it, I start becoming depressed again and I never want to go there again. So I have to be able to let my submissive side out. And my wife doesn't know how to draw it out, and I don't know how to let it out with her. So the only person that can draw it out is Mistress Jael, so the agreement with my wife is, whenever I need to see her, I see her, and my wife knows what happens. She struggles with the fact that, even though she knows no actual sex occurs, she knows it is a sexual experience. And she struggles with that. But at the same time, my wife does love me. She loves my vanilla me, very much. And I love and appreciate her for that. And she is trying to figure out, we are trying to figure out together, how can we make this work.

The most amazing thing about my wife, she's been trying to figure out what it means to be a dominatrix, and we've been trying to figure out ways to educate her, and so one of the ideas that I had come up with is that my wife try going to one of the domme classes that her sister puts on, so I broached that subject with my wife, and believe it or not, my wife is the only wife who has ever attended one of those classes. So she actually went two months, now there's no happy ending here because it was a horrendously bad experience for her. And this is where her conservative side, and where I feel really bad about my wife. One of the things we both realize is that we're trying to change the stripes on a zebra- she's not dominant. And one wouldn't necessarily have to be dominant, but she's not dominant and she's pretty sexually conservative. So she went to the class and we kind of misunderstood, and I was under the impression that it was going to be more conservative than it actually was. My wife is extremely shy in group settings, especially combined with sexual conservatism at a domme class. The first day was extremely difficult for her. She came home crying, trying to figure out whether she was going to go back the next day. Seeing women grab guys that they didn't know, grabbing their penises. I didn't realize how conservative she had become until she reacted this way to the class. It was really hard for me because I was torn between supporting her and trying not to be offended to her reaction to these things that I'm attracted to. She ended up going back the second day and came home crying and upset and so she didn't finish the third day. So the amazing thing is what she's trying to do to save our marriage.

I haven't even told her the entire list of things I like. I've started going through the list of things I'd like to experience, but it becomes so overwhelming for her that we haven't made a whole lot of progress. And it's not even that I need to experience all of those things, but I want her to know what it is that I find attractive so that she knows me. And we both have very busy lives and it's hard to set the time aside, to find alone time to actually have these deep conversations. So we're a work in progress. She has basically told me, we've both agreed that we don't know what the future holds, and that if it ends in divorce we will continue to love each other forever. There's no animosity. We both want each other to be happy in the long run. And she's even given me permission to date if that's what I need to do, and figure out what I want. Of course I haven't done that as of yet. The closest thing is I continue to see Mistress Jael very regularly, if not every week, every other week, and that's how I maintain my sanity. So we have an oddball deal, because I still have this hopeless romantic thing and I hate the exchange of money associated with all of this stuff. And because of our friendship and just my weird mental blocks, we've got a different deal. So I am helping her to develop a business, well I have developed a business for her, a business where we film our time together, tell the story, and with that I manage all of that, getting those videos online, do the marketing for her, and so she makes roughly 2000-3000 per month on that. And on top of that I pay her another 2000-3000 per month.

So I need to back up, Mistress Jael and I have made lifetime vows to each other. Not vows that can't be broken per se. We both agree that if I ever find what I need that she would allow me out of our contract, or if my wife was ever able to become my dominatrix or if she ever had a reason that she needed out. So ever since my emergence, we've become very, very close, and she almost has a second life with me. So we spend about, both as friends and as partners, Dominant-submissive partners, four hours a week on the phone, and that is just as friends, there's no D/s interactions on the phone, we're just talking as friends about life, and then together filming and D/s play, when we are in our modes, we're probably about five hours a week. So there's no penetrative sex – I've never been inside of her – there's no exchange of fluids, other than a golden shower, or champagne. And believe me, not for a lack of me wanting to, and she knows that, but she's in a relationship so that's the biggest barrier by far. So the typical session involves, that's really hard, because with this emergence, there's been this deep dive into D/s and submission. So I have gone from ten years ago, a year ago, she could ask me would I ever do anything forced bi, anything with a guy and I was absolutely no, that's a hard line for me, to two months ago I was tied down to a horse and taken anally by a man. I have sucked multiple cocks for her in the last year, because she kind of has a forced-bi thing, so she totally gets into that, and because she gets into it, it makes me want to get into it. I've never had any of those tendencies, and now I've done a lot.

So a typical session though, most common I'd say, I like everything, but I am a total, total bondage slut. So I like to be, I love to be completely immobilized, the more helpless I am the better. So my psyche, just so you understand my psyche best, where this grew from at a very early age, was because of all my sexual guilt, in my mind, sex was this bad thing, sin, don't do it, so very, very early on, my images of how I could touch myself, the images I'd play in my head to have some sexual satisfaction, were in my very early fantasies, being forced to do it, and it's not me touching me, it's a woman doing it. And she's forcing it on me and I'm tied up so I have no choice- so I'm not in the wrong here. So I very much like being in restrictive bondage, and she is a world-class restrictor. I also have a world-class collection of leather stuff. I'm not as much into rope bondage because I'm a leather fetishist. I like the act of being restrained, but I don't like spending the entire day doing an intricate rope scenario, it's more the psychological play and less the art form of the rope for example. I have also become a total, total ass slut, so very common to have strap on play, and because I've got this psychological thing, and I'm sure it's true for most subs, it's really important for me to feel she is getting off on it. For years I have researched ways to make it so she can orgasm while doing it. So we have many different methods, from she's figured out a way to put a really soft lipstick vibrator into her pants while she does it, to me finding dildos that have vibrators built into them that also tease her clit while she's doing it. So often times she can orgasm while we're doing it. Whether it's fake or not, I have no idea cause guys can't tell, but she says it's not so I take her at face value with that.

So I'm very highly visual, and because I'm a leather fetishist, I have built her up a world-class leather collection, and I also have my own leather outfits. And she's into that, she loves to play dress-up, so we both wear some very, very sexy type outfits when we play. I'm generally wearing a gimp outfit, but my body is looking so good these days she's wanting more of my body exposed. She loves talking about her hot cuckold. She doesn't like it when I put any kind of sexual pressure on her, like telling her, "God, someday I'd really love to be able to have sex with you." Those are just unwanted advances, so I've been trying to figure out a way to shut that down. So that's one of the ideas I came up with, because I realized I had this mental thing. If I was a cuckold, than I realized there was no way I was ever going to get that. So that's part of the play these days, it's been a recent thing. So restriction, lots of visuals, strap-on play, I really don't have limits in fact, again another major thing that has come out in me this last year, was I had never been a pain puppy. I mean I might be able to take a couple of swats with the paddle, and I'd be screaming and whimpering. But now she's brought that out in me because I know she likes it, and she has started to more and more, and because of this complete shift in my psyche, it's almost a badge of honor for me, and this is bad, only because I shouldn't allow my mind to be like this sometimes, but I love coming home every once in a while heavily marked. And not only wearing that badge of honor, but almost to shock my wife and for her to see:

this is very real, this is how deep it goes, and it's not just a
function of putting some leather on and having sex. Just recently,
about a month ago, she drew blood on my back. I probably took
about 70 strokes. I was marked for almost a month. Believe me, I
was crying real tears throughout the session, but that's how deep
I'd gone. And she was having a blast of course, pulling me down
the rabbit hole.

So we made lifetime vows together and she almost lives
this second life with me, and she admits it. She says, look we
have a real D/s relationship, we have written vows, and we're
filming it and it all works out great because it helps the business.
So not only that, but to the best of my knowledge, I've never seen
another dominatrix who's done it, but once again me diving deep
into the hole, there have been two major events in our
relationship: in December of last year when we made our vows to
each other, and June of this year, we had started talking about
some way, some mark, something I could wear for her, and one
thing led to another, and she'd never done it before and wanted to
do it, which made me want to do it, and in June of this year, I was
tied down, we both did all the research together, gagged, and she
gave me a Prince Albert, the cock piercing that goes through the
head of your cock, through your urethra. It's generally worn as a
ring that goes in your urethra and exits out the bottom of the
penis, just below the crown, about a half an inch from the tip.
Nothing to deaden the pain, nothing to do anything, it was all
very real. Right there. All on video. She pierced me. And we call
it, our wedding ring. So I wear that ring. I'm wearing it right now.
I wear it everyday. So of course I came home with that to my
wife, but I told my wife, this is one of those things I want to do.
My wife doesn't know what it means, because she really wouldn't
understand that and wouldn't accept it, so that's one thing I have
kept from her. But of course even though she knew what it was
going to be, when she saw it, she had a total break down when she
saw my back after a heavy whipping. She freaked out, and those
were the two times we came close to ending things right there.
And I tell her, when you have that repulsive reaction, it's showing
me that you don't love that side of me, that you can't accept that

side of me. But we've moved past those days, but again, we are in a "one day at a time" situation. And Mistress Jael and I will always be friends and I am so grateful to her for helping me love and live the suppressed me that I've suppressed my entire 47 years that literally my life today is completely different. What else can I tell ya? It's also brought out in me, I'm very much an alpha male, and when you put me in a setting with other men, I'm always vying for the lead, but my alpha male in a setting around women, died years ago. I mean literally, I wouldn't try to flirt, nothing, not since, a couple years after my marriage and I realized that I wasn't going to have with my wife. My wife and I have sex occasionally, and it's usually when we've been talking a lot, and we've been clearing a lot, and you just feel closer and that's usually what happens. So it's usually twice a month. What I've started to recognize about myself, and it's the one thing that still makes me sad that I struggle with every day is to try to refocus my life and myself in that. I've realized that neither of the two women in my life that I love can give me what I want or what I need in that what I've never experienced in my life is making love to somebody while I was submissive, and I can't have that with Jael, and I can't have it with my wife. It's okay. I just have to figure out that what I'm struggling with right now is trying to figure out how important it is to me. I'm trying not to suppress it. But I also recognize that first and foremost that woman who can do that is a needle in a haystack, and that's just a fact of life for a submissive male, it's what we go through. Because of the fact that it's so, so oppressed in our society, so as you know, women love to be submissive, and there are very few women who like to be dominant. And I honestly believe it's just because they haven't experienced it. So I recognize it's a needle in a haystack, number one, and number two, I realize that I am a beautiful, loving, caring, sexy, kinky sub and my hopeless romantic tells me that that needle is in the haystack somewhere. So these are the kind of things that keep me going from day to day. And that and me trying to keep my focus off of, Mistress Jael and I talk about this all the time, I mean my problems are so minuscule compared to people's problems, right? And I've really been working on hard lately to recognize how good my life truly is. For God's sake, I have a wife who lets me see, and sometimes orders me to go see my dominatrix. Because she says that I get grumpy and distant when I suppress too long and she tells me, "I want you to go see her this week." And we have an agreement that I don't tell her what happens because she doesn't want to know. Which bothers me because that is a suppression in and of itself. But that's her way of dealing with it and right now my life is day by day so I'll accept it, because I'm fortunate enough to have a wife who tells me to go see my Mistress. And there are people in this world who can't put food on the table. I'm very well to do, I'm very secure in my job, I make a lot of money and my job is not that hard. I have a family who lives a very healthy lifestyle, and on top of that, I provide very well for the other woman I love, for my Mistress.

This is another secret I'm going to tell you about, but she lives on the Westside, and she has a young daughter who's five, just started Kindergarten, and I know what that's like, having young kids, and she's my best friend, and watching her scramble everyday to get her to school, and still be a professional Dominatrix and drive downtown to the temple, so she hit me up. She owns the property at her house, she's got multiple rental properties, so she asked me would I go in on the rent for her rental space with her rather than renting it out, to make it our space, and I couldn't resist that, having a space that was a play space that I shared with her and more importantly could help her. The idea of her not having to drive all the way downtown for a session, that was my biggest driver. So as of about a month and a half ago I started pumping money into it left and right and it turned it into this operable, incredible play space. I came down there and actually hung sheet rock on the walls and spent several days with her. So again, she'd my best friend and you do what you can for your best friends. And also, I love her, and I'm very open with her about that, she knows that. She's one of the two women that I love in my life.

In a perfect world, if I could wave my magic wand and be with my wife and love her and make love to her and also be with Mistress Jael and love her and make love with her, and then to expand on that, it would be a perfect world. And, I've realized that I'm this deeply loving person, and Mistress Jael tells me this all the time, that I make her and the people around me feel very good. And she says, "You have a lot of love to give." And I want to give that love, but because of my strict Catholic upbringing, I've had very few relationships in my life, and I'm realizing there are so many beautiful people in this world, and people I'd love to get to know and to love.

I do realize that if I could feel like I was fully loved in a relationship, both my alpha side and my submissive side, then I wouldn't necessarily need to be poly-amorous, that 's the most important thing to me, I just want to be loved as a whole. But I'm realizing that I might never be able to have that, and I might have to experience it in another form.

I call my leather thing a fetish, but it's not a fetish in the true sense of the word. Mistress Jael and I were talking about this recently. I mean, I'm so attracted to her, I don't need to be tied up every single time, and she doesn't have to be head to toe in leather. I mean I have fantasies about her all the time, and I'm very open and honest about it, and most of those fantasies are vanilla, you know, making love to her in the shower, fantasies about being in a relationship with her. I've had many, many dreams about her, and she's always surprised by that, because she thought I had to have it all the time, but no I don't have to have it all the time.

For 47 years I have felt alone, like a freak. Like I was a bad person. And now I'm realizing how not alone I am. I am not even kinky compared to some, and I'm just blown away- people are so beautiful. And it's really helped me to be less judgmental about people, not even just about their kinks, but about life. I've transformed into a "live and let live" kind of person, which of course has led to some massive fights with my parents. They perceive me as becoming a heathen. Outside of Mistress Jael, you're the first person I've been able to share that with. And if my story helps anybody else, my life has been worth living. I don't want anybody else to live this suppressed life like I have. I don't want everybody to ever think they're ugly, because every single soul is beautiful. And that was the first thing that came to mind when I was told about the opportunity to talk to you. You know if anybody can gain from what you're doing, and from my story, and can hopefully help some 26 year-old kid not hate himself, that's worth it.

Closing Remarks

These interviews come from a research study that was conducted in the year 2017 to dispel myths about sex work and the men who seek it out, and to contribute to a more accurate understanding of male sexuality. Ultimately this research hopes to promote tolerance for both sex work and the varied expression of normal human sexuality, but to contribute to a sexual narrative for both sexes that widens the potential of how men and women express themselves sexually with one another. Male sexuality is not inherently deviant, violent, or lacking empathy, although many previous books have studies have tried to label it so, and the men who seek out sex workers are seeking connection and sexual expression that they could not find otherwise. Through understanding and illumination of the true nature of sexuality, one could hope to provide a new lens with which to view not only male sexuality, but the sexual dynamics between men and women, giving them permission to find more honesty and authenticity in their sexual expression both individually and with each other. In a society that values acceptance and understanding of individual sexuality, and the struggles humans endure to meet their sexual needs, one could hope to see more tolerance and understanding of sex in general, but also sex work, those who engage in it, and the true purpose it serves in society and for the individual. I hope that you've enjoyed their stories and that they have opened up a new understanding of male sexuality and sex work, and perhaps, more tolerance and acceptance of your own unique sexuality and sexual essence.

Lauren Brim, Ph.D.
Doctor of Human Sexuality

"There is no other greater ecstasy, than to know who you are."

- Osho